Ain't No Sunshine

MEN REVEAL THE PAIN OF HEARTBREAK

Compiled and edited by
Kimberley A. Johnson
and
Ann Werner

Also by Kimberley A. Johnson and Ann Werner

THE VIRGIN DIARIES

Also by Ann Werner

THE PEOPLE NEXT DOOR

Copyright © 2011 by Kimberley A. Johnson and Ann Werner

All Rights Reserved. No part of this book may be used or reproduced in any manner whatsoever without written permission, except in the case of brief quotations in critical articles or reviews.

Published in the United States by ARK Stories.

Cover design by Ralph Faust

This book is dedicated to anyone who's suffered a broken heart.

Acknowledgements

Thank you to all of the men who participated in this project. Your stories made us realize that men and women aren't so different after all. Thank you to Katherine Lurie, who suggested the idea. To Laura Stroube Hughes for her input and enthusiasm. To Ken Johnson for his suggestions and information. To Alex Lotterer for being our cover model. To Steve Baratz for his help and support. To therapists Dr. Stuart Jeanne Bramhall and Dr. Billy Lee Kidd, psychics Anne Temple and Madea-Michelle and perhaps the most front line of them all, bartenders Bob and Belinda.

I hold it true, whate'er befall:
I feel it, when I sorrow most;
'Tis better to have loved and lost
Than never to have loved at all.

Alfred Lord Tennyson
In Memoriam:27
1850

Dear Diary

I called him around 2:00 today. He didn't answer. I didn't leave a message. He always used to call me right back. It's 9:30 and nothing. I looked at his Facebook and he hasn't been on. He's probably on a date, having sex with some exciting NEW woman. Some stupid woman who doesn't yet realize that he's an ASS!!!!

This sucks! I HATE that I miss him. I wish I didn't think about him all the time. I wish I was stronger. I wish I was more like a man. They can just go out with someone else and it's no big deal.

Why isn't he calling me back???? I REALLY have to MOVE ON and NOT THINK ABOUT HIM ANYMORE!!! But I can't help it. Does he think about me? Does he even miss me? Tomorrow is the anniversary of our first date. I'll bet he doesn't even realize or care. Why do I even care???

I just wish that I knew if he was thinking about me. That I still mean something to him. Why isn't he calling me back? It's so much easier for men! It's NOT FAIR!!!

Introduction

Are men and women really from different planets? Do men experience things differently than women? Are men immune to the rush of emotions that sometimes plague women? After reading these stories, we've come to the conclusion that we're all from the same planet; we just don't speak the same language.

Women often assume that men have it easier after a breakup. They suspect that men will immediately go out on the prowl and thoughts of the lost love vanish from their minds as easily as yesterday's conversation at the water cooler. But is that really the case?

These are the questions that prompted us to create *Ain't No Sunshine*. We utilized the Internet and social media to reach out for answers. On these pages are the responses from men from all over the country—perhaps the world—who answered our questions about what it's like for them to go through the pain of heartbreak. The answers and the stories are sometimes surprising, always interesting and ultimately illuminating.

Do men cry? Do they sob? Do they call psychics? Do they drive by the house of the woman they've lost? Call and hang up? In short, do they do all of the things women do? We've got the answers! And these answers are straight from the horse's mouth, so to speak.

People tend to want to label us as experts. We're not. We like to say that we're expert at not being experts. What we are is curious and that curiosity has led to a unique collection of stories recounting how men deal with the loss of romantic love, whether the reason is death, betrayal, abandonment or just bad timing.

For fun, and to satisfy those who absolutely must have expert commentary, we've included observations from two therapists, two psychics and two bartenders.

It's also worth noting that throughout human history men have expressed their emotions through poetry and music. From William Shakespeare's *Romeo and Juliet* to Billy Ray Cyrus' *Achy Breaky Heart*, it's clear that when men have an outlet approved by society, they can be quite romantic and eloquent.

All of the stories are anonymous, which is key to getting an honest response. Without the fear of being ridiculed for admitting to being vulnerable, men dove right in and told us how they really feel. We bet it felt great for them to be able to unload in a public forum without actually going public!

The one disappointment we encountered while compiling this book was that we didn't get the number of gay stories we had hoped for. We tried, we really did, but the volunteers from the gay community were few and far between. Which makes the responses from those who did participate all the more appreciated.

Although we always ask people to change names and locations, we also realize that sometimes they get swept up in the tale they're recounting, so to be on the safe side we've changed all the names in the stories. Just want to make sure that anonymous really is anonymous!

As two women who have gone through our fair share of heartache and breakups, we both found what these men had to say not only fascinating and informative but also hopeful. From a woman's point of view, men are so often puzzling and vague. While these stories deal with heartbreak, they also provide a window into how men feel about love, family and commitment. It gave both of us new insights into the inner workings of men's minds and we think it will translate to you, the reader.

Enter here into the world of men who have suffered a broken heart.

Guidelines and Questions

You may use your own email address to reply or you may create a free one on yahoo, gmail or hotmail so that you can remain completely anonymous.

Please answer all the questions that apply to you in detail. You can arrange them into an essay or you can cut and paste the questions into an email and answer each one and we will arrange the story so that it flows and is easy to read. The only editing we will do is to clean up punctuation, remove repetitious answers and fix any grammatical issues.

Please do not answer with a yes or no. The key here is to understand what men go through and we are looking for a story. We will not accept any story that is gratuitously vulgar. Nor will we accept stories that have not followed our specifications. We will only ask for your story one time. If we feel it is something we wish to use we may email you asking about anything that was left out.

All stories will be anonymous. Please try to be as vague as possible about any personal information. For example, if you moved to another state to be with someone, do not mention the name of the state. You can say something like I moved 500 miles to be with her/him or I moved across country. Please do not mention a company where you or that person may work...substitute with their profession. Do not use the real name of the person you are writing about. We will change every name in the story in case you accidentally name someone.

By submitting your story, you agree to release all rights to Ark Stories and understand that the stories may be used in whole or in part for the purposes of publication, promotion and/or distribution in any manner. We make no guarantee that we will use your story.

We thank you in advance and are grateful for your contribution.

Age:

Sexual orientation:

Have you ever gone through one or more breakups that were devastating to you? Did the one you love pass away? If they passed away, please describe the circumstances.

How long were you together?

Were you married to any of these people and/or have children with them?

Why was the breakup so hard? Without revealing anyone's identity, why did you break up?

Did you try to get back together? Did you offer any promises that you had a hard time with prior to the breakup as a lure to get back together? For example: if you cheated and he/she left you, did you promise to be monogamous?

How did you express your pain? Did you cry? Sob? Did you mope? Call a psychic? Talk to a friend? Did you hide those feelings or did you allow anyone to know how upset you were? Please be specific and provide details.

How long before you began seeing other people? Did it help? Were you looking for another relationship or just people to date?

If you had sex with one or more people afterward, how long did it take and did it help? Did it make you feel better or worse?

What is the longest period of time it took you to get over someone? Is there someone you have never gotten over?

Did you ever:

    Call them and hang up?

    Drive by their home?

> Google their name?
>
> Snoop around their life through mutual friends?
>
> Spy on them using Facebook, Twitter or other social media?

What was the most embarrassing thing you feel you did?

Have you ever felt desperate or suicidal about a breakup?

Did you find out your ex met someone else before you did? How did that make you feel? DETAILS!!!

How long did it take for you to finally feel okay about it? How did you get to that point?

Has there ever been a person you fell hard for but never really got the chance to explore it? How did it make you feel? Were you depressed? What did you do to move past them?

Have you sought therapy to help you get over someone? What advice did you get? Did you apply it and did it work?

Is there something you wish you could say to any of your ex's or love interests that never came to be? What would it be?

For fun:

Do you believe in soul mates?
Have you met yours?
Do you think you can have more than one?

If you're not married, would you like to be and why?

Is there anything you would like to add?

44 Straight

I grew up in a small town. I kept to myself and was very shy. In December of my senior year in high school, "the new girl" entered my school, my grade, my life. I will call her Jessica. She was nothing like the girls from where I lived. A mix of mostly hippie, a little punk rock and some Stevie Nicks. Every guy in school was fascinated with her. She had an air of confidence that we had never seen. She used profanity and smoked cigarettes. The other girls hated her on sight, in part because she was sexy and beautiful but mostly because she commanded all the attention. I was smitten along with every other guy in town.

For some reason I will never understand, Jessica quickly took an interest in me. We sat together in science class and were paired to do an assignment together. We got homework and I felt like I had won the lottery. But I was also petrified. I wanted her to like me but I was so dull in contrast to her wild and exciting ways. I felt it best to just keep quiet and let her handle everything; this way I could look cool.

We made arrangements to meet after school and I invited her to my home. Both of my parents worked and I longed to be alone with her. Not because I thought we would have sex (I was a virgin) but I figured being alone with her could lead to a real relationship—and it did. We became inseparable. My parents were not happy. Her parents loved me. I think they hoped I would calm her down. I let them down.

For a year and a half I celebrated and endured the most bizarre, upsetting, exciting, crazy and exhaustive relationship of my life. I let her take me over. She said "Jump" and I asked "For how long? How high? Would you like me to add a skip?" I was a complete doormat for her. I put off college, which infuriated my parents. I fell out of my small circle of friends. My life was all about Jessica. I thought I was happy but looking back, I think I was always on the verge of tears. She stirred me and I think I always knew our time would be fleeting. I was always desperate for her, even when we were together.

I lost my virginity with her. She was not a virgin. She would say all these crazy romantic things to me about our love and future. She would plan out our wedding, talk about the kids we would have, how we would travel and lead an exciting and unconventional life.

We had been together for over a year. That February she became pregnant. I was secretly elated when she told me. I thought to myself, THIS would be how I would have her forever. We would

HAVE to get married now. I really believed for about five minutes that I had her locked in.

She told me she was going to have an abortion. I crumbled. Something inside of me knew right then and there that somehow she would be out of my life soon. It was awful. She had the abortion and afterward we cried together. She explained that even though we had discussed marriage and children, there was too much she wanted to do with her life. She wanted to travel, to live. I just sat back, listened to her and felt her slipping away.

In May she told me a group of friends invited her to stay the summer in France. She was supposed to come back in August. I argued with her; I pleaded with her not to go. I then offered to go with her. She told me that there wasn't enough room for me and this would be a good way for us to miss each other. By the time of her return, our love would be new again. There was no winning with her (at least where I was concerned).

I will never forget the day I took her to the airport. She was so happy and excited. I was a complete disaster. I was angry at her for being so happy and feared I would never see her again, despite her promises to write often. Because we were so young and had little money, we couldn't afford the long distance charges to speak on the phone.

I do not remember a darker day in my life than the day she left. I sat in the airport parking lot in my car for two hours and sobbed. I was weak and felt like I had no energy for anything. Even now, all these years later, writing this brings back the severe pain I was feeling. I am lucky I survived the drive home. I can barely even remember it. I was drunk with sadness.

> ***The hunger for love is much more difficult to remove than the hunger for bread.***
>
> *Mother Teresa*
> *quotegarden.com*

I wrote to her and she replied twice. Her letters proved that she was having the time of her life. I feared she would meet someone else. I feared everything and was angry. I resented the fact that I was too young to go there and bring her home. Then the letters stopped. August came and went.

I visited her parents and when her mom opened the door, I could see the pity she had for me. She told me that Jessica was staying on and planning to live there. I was crushed and defeated.

I cried, I sobbed; I felt so sorry for myself. The pain was so intense for so long. I went through two years of torture, waiting for her to surprise me. I withdrew even further and had absolutely no social life. My parents were concerned and insisted I go to therapy.

The therapist did help me. She let me talk and cry but no one could take the pain away. That took years. She had me write down my goals, she tried to encourage me to date other girls but I couldn't even think about anyone but Jessica. I was completely obsessed with her.

I can't put a number on how long it took me to get over her. Writing this out and thinking deeply about it brings it all up for me again. I do not feel devastated now. The last time I saw her I was nineteen years old. But I remember the pain I felt. I can feel that pain this second. It took me at least two years to get to the point where I felt somewhat normal. It took three years before I went on a date.

Over the years I have looked for her online. I've looked on Facebook and haven't found her. I admit to being curious but I think it would really be best if I never see or hear from her again. She had an unhealthy power over me. I'm not sure if she still would but I can sense that I might still be vulnerable. I am married now and quite content. My wife is more suited to me. We have a good life. I trust her and wouldn't want to put her through anything negative because of Jessica.

Jessica not only broke my heart, she ripped it into shreds. She made me feel so insecure and in the end, walked away so easily that I questioned if she ever really loved me.

I thought I loved her. But I was obsessed with her, infatuated. It was a crazy sick attraction. I longed to be close to her but I never felt I "got in." Therefore I felt like it was an unfair field. She was IN me. I was only about her and I think I was a part of her for a brief time until something else captured her attention.

Over the years I have wondered what I would say if I had the chance to see her again. I have thought to ask if she ever really loved me. Now I feel like it is best to let go. There is some weird grip she will always have. But not to the point where I feel pain. As I said, I love my wife and don't wish to break that bond.

I do believe in soul mates. I think Jessica was one, is one, but not THE one. I am not sure why she came into my life. Maybe to help me appreciate my wife in a way I might never have. My wife is the soul mate I wish to spend my life with.

39 Straight

I was married for twelve years to the love of my life. We have two young girls. My wife Linda was going on a job interview. She hadn't worked since before our first daughter was born. Jade was five and Casey was three. Linda loved working. She also loved being a mom. She decided to get a part time job, since her mother was able to watch the girls while she was at work. I encouraged her to do what she wanted but I was hopeful she would wait a few more years before going back to work. I didn't want her to regret her choice but she insisted.

Her interview was early in the morning. She was so excited to wake up early with me. She buzzed around, getting everyone breakfast and the girls ready to go to their grandmother's house. We kissed goodbye and she asked me what I wanted for dinner. I told her I would think about it and call her later. She told me she loved me and I told her that I loved her and wished her good luck and to drive safe.

Several hours later, I got a call from the police. My number was stored in her cell phone. Linda had been killed in a car accident. A drunk driver hit her while she was at a red light. I was told that the impact was so strong, the doctors believe she died instantly. I hope that is true. I hope she never saw it coming and never felt any pain.

It has been two years since she died. At first, I was unable to cope at all. I stayed in bed for a month. I took sleeping pills and shut myself off from the world. I see that as selfish. Linda's mother took care of the girls and I know the death was very hard on her. Linda was her only child. I simply could not function. I wept and grieved. It is all a blur to me because I barely left my bedroom. At times I still cry and cry hard. I do my best to keep things together for the girls but I ache daily.

At this point, I cannot think about being with another woman. I am still in love with Linda and I couldn't introduce another woman to my children. It's too soon and I feel it's wrong.

I wish everyday that anything would have been different. I wish we would have been running late or her car wouldn't have started. But these thoughts are not helping me move past this. I am not sure how to move past this but I have made some strides in these last two years. I can work. I must be strong for our daughters.

I have thought about suicide purely as fantasy. I would never take my own life because of my daughters. I could never do that to them. It is very hard raising two daughters as a widowed father. I fear what will happen when they reach high school. Will I be enough? Will I be able to guide them and help them have confidence? How will the loss of their mother affect the way they view themselves? I am fortunate to have Linda's mother to help me with all of this but she doesn't take the place of their mom. No one ever can.

> *No one can keep his griefs in their prime; they use themselves up.*
>
> *E.M. Cioran*
> *quotegarden.com*

I am considering therapy now. Up until this point, I have stayed away because I know I will have to relive everything. I will have to face what I have been shoving down inside. I know I could be a better father and need help to show me the way. I have not taken any antidepressants and hope not to, so I think a psychologist is best. To me, it's the harder way. Drugs cover up pain. I think you have to go through it to move away from it. I have been putting it off but I do think the time has come. I find it serendipitous that I happened upon your request for stories. I saved the questions for several weeks and have been putting that off as well. Today I decided to write it out. I would guess you want more detail than this.

I will say that I am in pain. I suffer every single day and I honestly don't know how I will continue. But I have a family I must care for and they are paramount. They are more important than me moping around.

I talk to Linda everyday. I feel she watches over all of us. I ask her for strength and for help when I don't know what to do. I hope that when I die, I can be with her again

Linda is my soul mate. I don't know if you can have more than one. Maybe.

47 Straight

I was dumped because of fake boobs.

I was with Kara for just over three years. Everything was fine. She had small breasts and a great body. I loved her and I thought she loved me. She DID love me. On our second year anniversary, I proposed and she said yes. We decided to wait for two more years. Her brother was in the military serving out of the country and was due back in two years, so we wanted him to be with us and share in the celebration. We had just moved in together so there wasn't any rush.

Her grandmother died and left her some money. She had always complained about the size of her breasts and wanted bigger ones. I tried to tell her time and time again that I thought she was beautiful and big fake tits were a waste of money but when she got her inheritance, off she went. She opted for a D cup. She went from an A to a D.

I was there for her. I hated that she did it but I figured if it made her happy, she would finally stop going on about how insecure she was.

Soon after she was totally healed, her confidence went through the roof. Suddenly she was wearing provocative clothing with a lot of cleavage and everything about her attitude changed. I tried very hard to allow her space. I thought that after a while, she would calm down. She was going out a lot more with her girlfriends. I would complain and she would snap at me that she was having fun. She said she felt good about herself and didn't want me to try and keep her down. I wasn't trying to keep her down; I just wanted her to realize she didn't need huge boobs to have confidence. I also wanted that newfound confidence to spill over to me. But it didn't. It was clear she was getting a lot of attention and loved it. She is petite and her breasts were enormous.

She completely shaved off all of her pubic hair. This was not the woman who I knew and I was worried and had good reason to be. But I still loved her. We still managed to have some of what we had before the breasts but she had changed.

Soon enough, she dropped the bomb. She announced she was breaking off the engagement and moving out. I was dumbfounded. I couldn't believe what she was saying to me. I almost didn't believe her but she packed up and left.

I found out through a mutual friend that she was dating a much younger guy. She was thirty-eight and he was twenty-five. I suspect this was going on while we were still living together, hence the shaved pubic area. I don't understand this look. Big fake breasts and a shaved pubis. It is not natural and not appealing, not to me anyway.

It was very hard for me. I still loved her despite her inflated ego and I really thought she would eventually get used to her new body and calm down. I'd hoped that all the attention she was getting would help her feel more confident in herself and our relationship. I tried so hard to be patient. I had been there for her through the loss of her best friend. I had helped her financially. But most importantly, we had agreed to spend the rest of our lives together. When she dumped me, I felt used and tossed aside as soon as she found something better. It made me feel like it was all a charade. I wondered if I really meant something to her. Did she only "love" me because I was the best she could do?

It really hurt.

I felt completely desperate and sorry for myself. I couldn't believe what happened. It was embarrassing to explain to people. "My fiancé got bigger boobs and left me for a twenty-five year old." I was humiliated. Then I got pissed. What kind of person treats another that way? She is shallow and not worthy of what I had to offer. Frankly, even though it was devastating and I really was hurt, I am grateful this all happened before I married her.

I cried a lot for about a month, give or take. Alone. I never cried in front of anyone. I drank too much and I was miserable. It felt like she sucked all the confidence I had out of me and injected it into those damned tits. This must sound funny, it actually made me laugh to write that but at the time it was true.

While I was in the midst of grieving my relationship, I didn't date anyone. My friends would try to get me out but I was too defeated. I wished at the time I had it in me to just go out and have sex with a woman but I was too busy feeling sorry for myself. She really did a number on MY self-confidence. I would ask mutual friends about what she was doing and that is how I found out she was dating a child.

It took half a year to finally wake up and realize I was better off without her. A year later I met the woman I married. I had some dates before I met her but by that time I was over Kara. My wife is my soul mate. I never really bought into that but there have been a few things that have made me a believer.

I realize I have a strange story and it will probably make some people laugh. I can laugh about it now and my friends are always making sure to supply me with fake boob emails, cards, you name it. But at the time, I was very hurt. I loved her enough to want to marry her and she rejected me. It caused to me to question myself in a negative way. I have always been confident. Not cocky. Not arrogant and I have always treated women with respect. It would have been easy for me to change that and take what happened to me with Kara and become bitter.

Eventually I realized that despite the fact I loved and wanted to marry her, she changed. It was about her, not me. I would lie in bed at night and cry myself to sleep thinking about what had happened. Because of the nature of why she left me, people generally tended to laugh. Initially I said she and I weren't getting along and had a big fight to avoid explaining what really happened. I wouldn't wish the pain and insecurity I felt on anyone.

> **In 2010 surgeons performed 296,203 breast implants, a 2 percent increase over 2009 and a 39 percent jump since 2000.**
>
> *New York Times: Health*
> *April 9, 2011*

34 Straight

I had a girlfriend in high school, Jenny. We met when we were both sixteen. We started out as friends but it didn't take long for us to be joined at the hip. We fell hard in love. I loved her so much it hurt. If we weren't together, we were on the phone. Every morning, we called each other before school. I wrote to her during my classes. On the weekends, we were together as much as we could be. Our parents were concerned that we were spending too much time together but never forced us to stop.

We were together for about two years. One night when we were eighteen, we went to a party. We both had a little too much to drink. When it was time to leave, she said she thought I was too drunk to drive and wanted to call her parents to come pick us up. There was no way my young male ego was going to let that happen. We had an argument and I won. I felt fine. I didn't feel sloppy drunk. She was angry but I wore her down. I will never forget what she said to me. "If I die, it'll be on your head."

I ran a stop sign and her side of the car was hit by an SUV. We both passed out from the crash. I woke up in the hospital. Both of us had been wearing seatbelts. My injuries were fairly minor. She was in intensive care. Both of our parents were there.

When I was made aware of her condition, a wave of guilt came over me that was overwhelming. I got sick to my stomach. Her parents were beside themselves with worry and extreme anger toward me.

Jenny was in intensive care for fifty-three hours and then she lost her battle to live. The day she died was so awful for me. To this day, I am not over it. I blame myself completely and I am not sure if I will ever get over what I did.

I have been in therapy on and off for years. My therapist focuses on the fact that I was young and did what so many others do at that age but there is no relief in that for me. Therapy has not helped. I take antidepressants and although they help, nothing will ever fix what I have done.

It has been sixteen years since it happened and it feels as fresh as the first week. I cannot forgive myself. There is a part of me that doesn't want self-forgiveness. Not only did I kill someone else's child, I killed the only woman I have ever loved.

She haunts me all the time. I dream about her at night. I seem to be caught in a loop of her memory. I play it over and over, remembering things we did. Places we went. Our dreams and hopes as a young couple.

I have considered suicide on many occasions. The guilt is monumental. I am not sure I will ever go through with it but I have many fantasies about how I would do it. Taking the antidepressants seems to curb that desire. Logically I feel like there is no point. Like if I were to take my own life, I would be committing another sin and it would take away the chance for us to reunite after I die.

I often wish I were dead.

I have not been with a woman since Jenny. I do have a job, a life and friends. My friends are worried about me. They want to see me happy and in love. I am simply not ready to open myself up to that. I hope that one day I can be open.

When I dream of Jenny, she is never angry. She tells me she loves me and that she is waiting for me. I never know if those dreams are real visits from her but even though I feel sad when I have them, they make me feel closer to her.

When it first happened, I didn't cry for the longest time, maybe a year. I was in shock. I withdrew from everything. I had planned to go to college and never did. When I finally cried, it seemed I couldn't stop and I cried for a long time every day.

Sometimes I cry now but it isn't as frequent. Mostly I have a dullness that I try to stuff down in order to deal with everyday life.

I have not taken a drink since that day and I never will again. The pain that I have dealt with since the accident has been life altering for me. It has stopped me from allowing myself to enjoy anything. The few times I have felt any happiness, guilt quickly takes over.

Teen alcohol use kills about 6000 people each year, more than all illegal drugs combined.

(Hingson and Kenkel, 2003) Full cite: Hingson, Ralph and D. Kenkel. Social and Health Consequences of Underage Drinking. In press. As quoted in Institute of Medicine National Research Council of the National Academies. Bonnie, Richard J. and Mary Ellen O'Connell, eds. Reducing Underage Drinking: A Collective Responsibility. Washington, DC: The National Academies Press, 2003.

MADD.org

I am not sure how I can allow myself to let any love in. At this point in my life, I am thinking about that possibility. I carry a lot of baggage. I don't even know if I can do it.

I love Jenny and wish I could rewind and have a chance to do it again with what I know now but life does not give you that chance. I wonder what I am doing here if all I do is hold myself back from anything good. Jenny was a happy, loving soul and I can imagine she would tell me to find a way to forgive myself. This is a battle I struggle with daily.

I am so sorry for what I did to Jenny, to her parents. I don't know how to forgive myself. I really want to.

I also hope that after I die, I can be with the only woman I love.

38 Straight

My wife left me to be with her boss. This sentence has caused me such anxiety and embarrassment.

> ***75% of men and 65% of women admit to having sex with people they work with.***
>
> *brokenheart911.com*

I was married for five years to a beautiful woman and lived "the life." I'm a successful man. I usually put in seventy-hour workweeks, which enables me to provide a very comfortable lifestyle. I do it for me but I also did it so my wife could work only if she chose to and she did choose to work.

One day, I came home from work to find my wife packing her stuff. She announced she was leaving me in a very matter-of-fact way. She wasn't cold. She just gave me the information. I stood there stunned. I had not seen this coming. I asked her what the hell she was thinking.

She told me she didn't love me anymore and she was sick of being treated like a trophy. WTF?? I had NO idea what she was talking about. I tried to talk to her, tried to get her tell me what was really going on. Whenever I asked her questions, she would reply with information about the separation. She informed me that she opened a new bank account, had filed for divorce and rented an apartment. She explained that this could be very neat and clean if I just faced facts quickly and didn't fight her on this. There was no way I could convince her to change her mind so it would be best to accept, comply and allow her to move on. I have to admit this really pissed me off. She treated me like I was a kid and she had a slightly condescending tone.

Not too long after she left, I found out she moved in with her boss and quit her job. I guess he supports her just fine. This was jarring for me. I felt humiliated. I have always been what is described as an "alpha."

I loved her. I know I could have been more affectionate. I know she wanted me to be more communicative but she knew who I was when we married. We dated for two and a half years before we got married and lived together for a year and a half. There were no surprises. I liked our life. We were together a total of seven and a half years.

The breakup was so hard because I loved her and because she took something away from me. She took away some of what I consider to be my masculinity. She was with another man while she was sleeping in the bed we made together. The thought of her having sex with me while she was making love to another man has really messed with my ego. Her leaving me has made me question who I am.

When we were married, I cheated on her twice. Both times with different women who meant nothing to me. It was easy. I was away on a business trip. I knew I wouldn't get caught and I was not emotionally attached. I never felt guilty about it. Now that I have been cheated on, I look at what I did with different eyes. My two "affairs" were purely sexual. Hers was emotional. This is why I am so—I don't know the word. I am hurt. I am angry but I am shocked.

It is bad enough that she left me the way she did. That was awful. But she found a way to hurt me time and again. Every time people ask why I am divorced (and they ALWAYS do), I have to tell them my wife left me. If I try to get away with something more vague and they find out the truth, I look weak. So I say it matter of fact. I leave out that she left me for her boss. But trust me, telling people that she left me at all is a knife through my chest each time. It tells people I somehow failed. I have NEVER failed at anything before.

She and I have never sat down and discussed what she meant by saying she was sick of being a trophy. I can only surmise that she feels like because she is beautiful and because I work a lot, that somehow I took her for granted. Maybe I did. It is almost a year since the divorce was final. I have thought a lot about how I conducted myself in our marriage. I was not there much. I worked and when I played, I played with the guys: golf, camping etc. Now I question my ability to really be there for someone else.

I did call her several times after she walked out. I tried to get her to talk to me but she cut me off. I offered to go to a counselor. I told her I would make more of an effort. When I found out she had cheated on me, my effort to get her back stopped immediately. I then became angry and resentful. I am still angry.

I never cried. I try to keep busy. I have had a lot of dreams. The dreams are about her sometimes, that we are together and she loves me. I dream that I try to get her back and she accepts but then I remember what she did and I am angry. I have dreamed on more than one occasion that she chops my penis off. I guess we don't need Freud to analyze that one. My feelings are hurt and there have been times I have wanted to cry but the tears never came.

I have dated a few women but nothing serious. I can see, now that I have been cheated on, I am not entirely fond of the idea of getting involved again. Time will tell.

I have had sex. It has been ok. Not amazing. It's just sex. I keep detached and make the effort to treat it as something recreational. I am still working through my divorce.

I don't want her back. She left me for someone and I cannot look at her with love. I do wish that I could have prevented it somehow and rewind to a time when we were happy. I know I was happy and she had to have been. She has told me so little; I'm not sure what she thinks.

To me, calling and hanging up, driving by where she lives, trying to find out about her on the Internet or through friends and acquaintances is a serious waste of time. I am not obsessed with her. I am humiliated and feel like she stole something from me. She stole some of my confidence. I try to look at that as a lesson but I am still angry that she is happy and I am left to figure out what the hell I did or didn't do.

The most embarrassing part of all of this is admitting to people that I was left. I never felt desperate or suicidal and never felt the need to seek therapy. I'm still not over getting dumped but I'm working on it.

I have tried to talk with her but she kept our conversations brief. Sometimes I want to cuss her out. I guess I have nothing to say to her.

28 Gay

When I was twenty-three, I met Dave. I liked him a lot and I could tell he was gay—gaydar, I guess. It didn't take too long for us to find our way to each other sexually. I was a virgin and had not had sex at all with either sex. Needless to say, both of us enjoyed it very much. I told him there was no way I could let anyone know about what we had done. My family would disown me. As much as I hate this about them, my family is very important to me. We agreed to keep our relationship a secret.

As time went on, our feelings for each other grew into love. Everyone knew us as best friends. And we were.

After about a year, he started asking me about coming out. I could not even entertain this notion. The thought of having to choose him over my family was very stressful. I would explain this to him. He had come out to his family but they lived in another state. They initially had a tough time but eventually accepted who he was. He tried to convince me that my family would do the same. But I knew he was wrong. I had heard comments growing up of what my father thought of gay people and there was no way he would accept his only son being gay.

Our relationship continued for another year but it was always an argument about me coming out. He even said we could move to another state but the work I did kept me where I was. Where I am. I also think if I chose to move, people would still manage to find out.

This caused a lot of arguing between us. It got to the point where he gave me an ultimatum. He said, "You either love me or choose to live in your own hell." That really hurt me. I know he understood my torment but I felt it was very harsh for him to say that to me. He broke up with me. We were together for two years.

The breakup is devastating to me on so many levels. He is the only person I have been in love with. The only person I have been sexual with. Being gay and in a religious family that hates gay people is more difficult that I can explain. I miss him so much. I was and am so torn. If I choose to be gay, I lose my family. If I choose my family, I live a lie.

I tried and tried to convince him to stay with me. He explained that he could not live his life the way I was living mine and that if we were a couple, he would be living that lie too. I cried and begged but eventually he moved out of state and I have not heard from him.

I cried. I sobbed. I feel so alone and I question everything about my choice. I am angry at him and myself and my family. I don't see how to win this. I deal with this every day. Not just the pain of missing him, which is still alive, but the pain of my sexuality.

I have dated women to keep up appearances. But no men. There is a woman I see from time to time. She is nice and I like her but not in any sexual way. I think she suspects my sexuality but has not said anything.

It has been three years and I am still dealing with the pain. I constantly think about him. Every day of my life I want him back.

I have looked for him on Facebook but I haven't found him.

I guess that I am embarrassed because I don't know how to find the strength to admit to the world who I really am.

I have felt very desperate but not enough to kill myself. Though I often wish I would just die. Then I wouldn't have to deal with this anymore.

> **I'd rather be black than gay because when you're black you don't have to tell your mother.**
>
> *Charles Pierce*
> *quotegarden.com*

I wish I had the guts to tell him I am willing to live as a gay man. I am not sure if I will ever get there.

I do believe in soul mates and he is mine.

I would not want to marry a woman. I am afraid that I will allow my family to bully me in that direction for fear of being exposed. I am sure they wonder about me but I do my best to always have an excuse or say I date.

The Observation Deck

Psychiatrist

Dr. Stuart Jeanne Bramhall
Board Certified Psychiatrist
Practicing for 32 years

My experience is that women have vastly more emotional resilience in dealing with romantic heartbreak. Although women typically go through a profound grieving process, often accompanied by severe depression and suicide ideation, most have the ability to work through the grief in about six weeks or so and go on with their lives.

I have found that many men simply don't have the coping skills to do this. When they become suicidal following a breakup, it can go on for months or years—in essence, until they find another woman to replace their loved one. Some are at high risk for lethal suicide attempts—via hanging or shooting themselves—which are often successful.

I believe the basic problem relates to society's failure to socialize men to look after their own emotional needs. They are socialized to expect women to look after these needs (to mother them, in essence). Moreover, women tend to be socialized to look after their male partner's needs. What I find in working with couples is that women pursuing demanding careers simply get too stressed out juggling the demands of work, children and a needy partner—and that this is the chief cause of many breakups.

My experience with gay men is that they tend to have a lot more resilience than straight men. In the first place, they rarely go into a relationship with the expectation that their partner will "mother" them. Plus many of them tend to naturally develop the typical "feminine" skills of self-identifying feelings and emotional needs, of seeking and eliciting emotional support when it's needed and of various self-soothing techniques.

The men who come to see a psychiatrist following a breakup are not really in a position to benefit from advice. Most need to be started on antidepressant medication to keep them from killing themselves. Some, especially those who are drinking heavily, need to be hospitalized while waiting for the antidepressant to take effect.

Once the antidepressant starts working, therapeutic work can begin. What I find as a female psychiatrist is that I temporarily replace the loved one in a nurturing; mothering role, while the client gradually learns new coping strategies. It is not uncommon for men in this situation to have no friends of their own and no social outlets outside the marriage. I find that older men, especially, have left it totally to their wives to organize their social lives for them.

Thus this is usually the first thing we focus on—supporting a client who has never gone out by himself socially (or who stopped when he married) in venturing out into the community to form new relationships. What seems easiest for most men is to take some kind of adult education class or to join a hobby group (usually around outdoor activities). This can be very anxiety provoking for some men and often the outing is preceded by role playing in the office and developing a repertoire of small talk for interacting with new acquaintances. Sometimes grown children or siblings or other extended family members can facilitate this process and where possible, I engage them in the treatment.

I once worked with a forty-five year old man who refused voluntary hospitalization for depression and suicide ideation. His family (brother and sister-in-law) didn't want him committed and agreed to take him in and to do a suicide watch to keep him from killing himself. He began drinking heavily and snuck out to the barn in the middle of the night and hung himself. The man had no prior history of depression or alcoholism.

In cases where the breakup triggers a major depressive episode, usually antidepressants are necessary to prevent a suicide attempt. Once the depression comes under control, the first step is making sure the man has an adequate family and social support network. This usually involves going out and meeting new people, which many men find very difficult. Once basic social and support needs are met, cognitive behavioral therapy can be helpful in teaching men to identify and look after their own emotional needs, rather than relying on women for this.

Men confide all the time that while they are aching, they have sex with partners they aren't really interested in other than for the sex. It seems to help relieve some of the emotional pain and it's a lot safer than alcohol—which can be deadly in men in this situation who are depressed and suicidal.

35 Straight

I am a Marine.

I was with my girlfriend Melissa for about two years when I was called to go to Iraq. Before I left, I bought Melissa an engagement ring. I proposed and she said yes. I knew I wanted to marry her months before I got the ring. I thought if I made it official, I would have a deeper motivation to stay alive.

Melissa was my best friend. I met her when I was working as a bartender. She would come into the bar where I worked with her friends and we had an instant connection. She was so pretty. Long blonde hair, big brown eyes and the most beautiful lips I had ever seen. I tried to act cool around her but inside I was a mess. I wanted her so much but I was shy.

One night she came into the bar alone. It was a slow night and we had a chance to really talk. I finally got up the nerve to ask her on a date. For me, the first date was the start of us being together forever. I was twenty-five and she was twenty-three. She made me work for her affections and I was happy to.

Before I left, she told me she was scared. I told her that we would email and write and that I needed her strength and prayers. I wanted to come back and marry her, start our life and our family. We planned to have a big family—at least five kids.

It was July. I had been there for seven months. It was a hard month. Very hot and two of my good buddies died. I had also learned that my grandmother passed away and that made me sad. I was very close to her and it killed me not to be at her funeral. It wasn't long after that I got the email from Melissa. She told me she needed to break our engagement. She wrote she couldn't be engaged to me anymore because the time and distance were too much for her. Reading the email was surreal. I didn't know what to think. All these macho Marines surrounded me and I had to play it cool but I wanted to curl up and die. I wanted to cry. But I couldn't.

That night when I went to bed, I cried very quietly. My best friend over there heard me and asked me what was going on. He was the only person I talked to about it. He did help me. He let me cry. There is something about being in a war. Men seem to bond in a way they don't when you're just friends at home having BBQ's and drinking beers. There was one time when I completely broke down and sobbed. He held me. I am sure a lot of the guys would have seen that as gay but

I was such a wreck. He was there for me and I will never forget it. I definitely felt suicidal in the beginning. I hoped that I would get shot or something. My buddy was there the whole time and I credit him for keeping me alive. I wanted to be careless.

I didn't even tell my family about it for a month. I was humiliated and embarrassed. I didn't want to answer questions. I emailed Melissa many times. I tried calling her and writing her letters but she never replied.

When I returned to the States, I found out Melissa was with another guy. Many of my friends knew this but never told me. Looking back I am glad. It was hard to go through that. Being over there, not knowing if I would be around tomorrow, seeing people die—all for a war I didn't believe in. I take pride in being a Marine. I would gladly fight and die for my country but we weren't fighting for our country. I won't get into it here but what I saw was very corrupt.

I haven't admitted this to anyone but for about a week after I was dumped, I took my anger and frustration out on "the enemy." I was vicious. I was mean. It stopped when I realized that I was starting to become something I thought was evil. I am not an evil person. But I was so hurt and angry; I guess I thought if I could release it to the enemy, I could find some peace. It only made me feel worse. The whole rest of the time I was there, I hoped that I would hear from her telling me she changed her mind and wanted me again.

> *One should rather die than be betrayed. There is no deceit in death. It delivers precisely what it has promised. Betrayal, though...betrayal is the willful slaughter of hope.*
>
> *Steven Deitz*
> *thinkexist.com*

I saw Melissa a short while after my return home. We ran into each other in the store. We went to the parking lot. She seemed cold and scared. I was still very hurt and I asked her all these questions. Mostly "Why?" Why did she do this to me? Didn't she love me any more? All she could say was that she was sorry and ran to her car. It kind of brought it all up again for me and I felt like I had been dumped again. I did seek therapy both because of Melissa and my time at war. It did help. I was given Prozac and after a while, I was able to calm down and not feel so alone.

I have looked her up on Facebook but she has a private profile so I can't really see anything. I never drove by her house or called and hung up. I didn't even call to talk to her when I got back. When I found out she was with someone else, I had too much pride. I did cry a lot at first but after a few months, I was able to get past it.

During that time I wasn't dating anyone and didn't have sex either. I could have but I chose not to. I felt it would be too tough, that I would only compare her to Melissa.

I started dating and eventually started seeing a woman regularly. We aren't together anymore but the breakup was not devastating. We just didn't click. Right now I am dating a little and would like to find a woman to marry. I just put an ad on a dating site so we'll see. I hope that what happened with Melissa helps me and doesn't hurt me. I don't want to allow that pain to color my next relationship.

There was a long time when I wanted to say hurtful things to Melissa. I wanted to hurt her because I was in so much pain. I never did and I am grateful. I know that wouldn't have helped her or me. Now I would just wish her well. I hope she understands what she did was cowardly and selfish and that breaking up with someone while they are at war is one of the most devastating things to do. I guess there is never a good time but that was a real low blow.

I believe if you find the right mate, someone who fits with you, it's maybe what people call soul mates but I am not sure if I think that is all really true. I thought Melissa was mine but I guess I was wrong. I do know I can love someone, though, and I really want to.

44 Straight

Fourteen years ago I went through a breakup I never saw coming. It was extremely devastating. We'd been together for four years and were engaged to be married. We had no children.

I came home one night and she was passed out on the couch after having drunk a bottle of Cask and Cream. On the table in front of the couch was a small note that read "I am leaving, please don't ask me why." To this day, I have never known the reason.

During our relationship, she broke up with me but she said she just needed some space. After three months we ran into each other again and went out to dinner. I explained exactly how I felt about her and told her the most precious thing I ever had was her heart. We got back together and she knew I wanted to spend the rest of my life with her.

The night I read the note, my stomach just fell to the floor and I went numb. The night she actually left, coming home was the worst experience I have ever felt. We rented the upstairs half of an older Victorian home that was refinished. When we moved in we took over the finishing and completed it together. When I walked in the door to go upstairs, there was a haunting empty echo that rang throughout the unit and just tore through my heart. I knew going upstairs to an empty apartment was going to hurt like hell. I walked through the apartment remembering all the time we spent painting and stenciling out the walls and doorframes. In the dining room we use to make French toast at 9pm and play cribbage. No matter where I went, I could see what we had done from time to time and the thought of her leaving just tore me up so bad that it took years to overcome. I looked out the living room window towards the town and decided I could not be in this apartment anymore, so I went to the bar and for the next seven years decided that I was going to die drunk and numb. Something like from the movie *Leaving Las Vegas*. During that time I made some drinking friends but never got close to anyone again. I was asked once why I drank so much and my only response was I just didn't care.

She left me fourteen years ago and I have never slept with anyone since. Making love with the one you truly love is something I just can't explain. To have sex with someone else would just feel empty: no meaning or point to it. Don't get me wrong, I'm not gay and never will be. I just don't feel what I used to feel anymore, so to try to recapture that would most likely do more harm than good. I started to kind of date an old friend but that didn't last very long. We are still close friends but as far as dating, I just quit.

The time I was going through this, I was just a tough guy who could handle anything you threw at me as long as I had a bottle of rum. And yes, it worked.

> **The first thing in the human personality that dissolves in alcohol is dignity.**
>
> *Author Unknown*
> *qoutegarden.com*

It took seven years of drinking to get over her. I came home from the bar one night and for some reason, everything came flooding back all at once. I wasn't ready or able to deal with it. I remember thinking that I actually understood why some people would commit suicide. Understanding why people kill themselves was not a good thought at that time. I had given up on any hope. I lost who I was as a person: my sense of humor, self worth—everything. I would never have the balls to pull the trigger but if the alcohol didn't do me in, I guess there was a reason for it.

I am not a religious person by any means but that night I had to know. To have that much of you taken away—I asked for what reason? I asked whomever—angel or God or whomever. I said that I understand the pain of losing someone. With any loss, it will hurt. I didn't have an answer to that because she never told me why. I just wanted to know why. At that very moment I understood why. I didn't have the actual answer but I understood and it was like what they say, a huge weight was lifted, it actually felt like that. From that point on I decided to find myself again. Even so, every single day I wish I could have her back.

I decided to look her up after two and a half years. She was involved with someone and the sight of me really freaked her out so I left. I realized that sometimes in order for someone to be happy, it might not involve you being in that picture. I really wish her nothing but the best and to be happy. It took ten years for me to accept it and to be able to move on. Every day it still hurts and will probably hurt until I die. You just learn to live with it and maybe help others along the way so they don't end up making a fatal mistake. I just wish her all the happiness in the world because when she was happy and smiled, it could melt the world. She has, and will always have, the most beautiful smile I have ever seen.

As far as someone I fell for but never had the chance to explore those feelings, there was one girl in school I really had the hots for but if I had let anyone know I liked her, she would have never been able to live it down. I was more of the school clown back in those days. Now, thirty years later, we had a chance meet on Facebook and have been friends ever since.

I thought I found my soul mate but now I don't think there is such a thing. I really wanted to be married. Never did it. I realized that a person can be happy without having a relationship. Just remember what makes you happy: camping, movies, perhaps music?

Even though some scars may never heal, if I could go back and change everything, I would not. That night when I was asking those questions to whomever, the answer made me see something. Everyone wonders why God would allow suffering. This question has been asked for many years without any answer, just confusion. My suffering has opened my eyes and I want to share with others that have given up all hope or any chance of it. To be able to restore just that one little piece of hope, if even for only a moment, it might just be enough for them to keep fighting instead of giving up. So my answer to why does God allow suffering would be this: to teach us compassion and understanding.

To this day I am still single and have no plans on getting involved any time soon. I have found happiness again and have been putting myself back together. I quit drinking five years ago and quit smoking two years ago, so I am doing ok.

47 Straight

I am married and have been for twenty years. When my wife and I got married, I was in love. We had a baby and for a long period of time I was happy. About seventeen years into the marriage, I started to feel like I didn't want to be there anymore. I loved my wife but I was no longer "in love" with her. Frankly, I was bored. Our child was seven. I wasn't sure what I was going to do.

I work for a large company and I met a woman there. I only saw her from time to time but the day I met her, I liked her. She was totally different. She is sharp, funny, pretty and there was a spark between us. I worked with her and as we got to know each other, we found we had so much in common. She made me laugh. That is big. My wife used to make me laugh. I started thinking more and more about this coworker. I looked for reasons to call or email her. We would talk and laugh and I was starting to have real feelings for her. Four or five months passed and our relationship deepened. She had a boyfriend so in a way, I felt safe.

In the summertime, my wife and kids went out of town. I was alone for a week. My new friend told me she and her boyfriend broke up. We were at the office late and decided to have dinner together. I knew I was playing with fire but I couldn't help myself. I was so drawn to her and felt like I was falling in love. I did feel very guilty but that didn't stop me.

At dinner, we had drinks. My heart was pounding through my chest. I had never cheated on my wife but I think I would have killed someone to be with that woman. We stretched dinner out for as long as we could. In the parking lot, we stood at her car and talked for about fifteen minutes and then we kissed. I could literally see fireworks. My stomach was doing flip-flops. She said softly " I want you." We went to her place and spent the night together. I can honestly say it was the best sex I've ever had. Not because it was forbidden, but because she was amazing. It felt to me like we were meant to be together. Everything we did felt perfect. She instinctively knew what to do, how to touch me. We made love for hours.

The next morning, I was a mixed bag of love, guilt, fear and confusion. I needed to get out of her place but I didn't want to look like an ass. So I told her I needed to help a friend move.

I went home and freaked out. I took a sleeping pill and slept the whole day. When I woke up, I called her. Told her I wanted to see her again. We did see each other three more times that week. We had sex, went to dinner and played. By the end of the week, I knew what I had done was an awful betrayal of my wife. I couldn't be married to her anymore. I didn't love her. I wasn't sure what would happen with this new woman but I knew I didn't want my wife.

My wife called me the day before she came home and told me she had a surprise for me. This made me feel terrible. I had been cheating on her and she was planning to surprise me. When she got home, she informed me she was pregnant. My heart sank. We rarely had sex at all. When we do, we don't use any birth control. She was excited. I was devastated. I couldn't leave her like this.

When I went back to work, I told the new woman my news. I could tell she was upset but she remained cool. Not too long after, she found her way to another office and now we don't have much contact. Sometimes we run into each other at meetings. I think about her all the time and feel like I should be with her. But I also question if what I feel for her is because I want what I can't have.

There isn't a day that goes by that I wonder what may come in the future. I recently found out she is living with a man and I took the news very hard. Don't get me wrong, I love my children and I have a kind of love for my wife but I don't have any excitement for her anymore. I go through the motions. I am the dad, I go to work, I buy Christmas presents. But I always think of the other woman. She has my heart and it feels like she always will.

I never pursued her after that one week together. I had nothing to offer her. I pushed my pain deep down, though I think of her every night before I go to bed. I think of her when I have sex with my wife. There have been times while driving to work I start to cry. But not a lot. Can't go to work with a red nose.

I have not been with another woman other than my wife. She was the one affair I had and I don't believe I will ever allow that to happen again. It has been two years and I am still not over her.

I don't wish I could get her back. But I do wish things had happened differently. This also makes me feel guilt. I love my baby but if my wife had not told me she was pregnant, I would not be married now.

I never did things like calling and hanging up or see if I could find out what she was doing through mutual friends but I did drive by her house and Googled her name. I look at her Facebook page. I can see her wall and pictures. I saw a picture of the man she is with now and it makes me feel physically ill.

The most embarrassing thing for me is that I cheated on my wife. I never told her because I knew I was going to stay with her. If I told her, I know she would have been destroyed.

I am not sure I feel okay about it. It eats at me daily but I just have to sleep in the bed I made for myself. I made a commitment but I stay because of our children. I wish I could tell her that I think she is the one I am supposed to be with but what is the point?

> **Cheating spouse statistics confirm that between 50 and 70% of married men (between 38 and 53 million men) have cheated or will cheat on their wives. One study found that two thirds of the wives (26 to 36 million women) whose husbands were cheating had no idea their husbands were having an affair—largely because they failed to recognize the telltale signs.**
>
> *brokenheart911.com*

28 Straight

I have gone through a couple of difficult breakups but the one I went through in the Fall of 2010 has hit me quite hard. I was with a woman for just over a year. I fell for her as soon as I saw her. Right from the start we hit it off. We saw each other every day and quickly became a couple. Soon after, we talked about getting married and having a family.

I noticed she pulled away from me in the last months we were together. At first it was just a little bit but it increased. She spent more time away from me and I was getting the feeling that she was making up excuses and saying she was busy to avoid being with me. It really bothered me and I didn't know what to do about it. I was afraid to bring it up because I thought she might end it.

I stepped up my game. I planned romantic evenings and sent her flowers at work. She didn't even acknowledge getting the flowers until I asked if they arrived.

I finally got the courage to ask her what was going on and she told me what I really didn't want to hear and then some. She told me she wasn't in love with me anymore and she wasn't sexually attracted to me. She said she felt bad and that she tried to wait it out to see if maybe she could get those feelings back but the feelings were no longer there for her anymore.

It hurt a lot to hear that. I tried to stay calm and asked what we could do and her answer was that she wanted to break up. She started crying and I knew her tears were real. She wasn't being a bitch and that almost made it worse. She told me she had been in love with me and couldn't give me a reason why she wasn't anymore. As she cried, I cried. It was a weird moment. We were both so sad. I thought to myself, if we both felt so sad about things ending, why did they have to end? I asked her and she said, "They just do. At least for now."

So I had no choice. We broke up.

It has been very hard for me because I still love her and I can't do anything about it. It's been about four months. I want her back so much. I keep waiting for her to call me and tell me she was wrong or confused. I think about the life we had. On Sunday mornings, we would make a great breakfast. We would save that day for us and be totally indulgent. Eat, sex, wine. Whatever we felt would make us happy. Now Sundays are the worst for me. I wake up and I realize that it's another one without her. I hate Sundays now!

I have called her a number of times. I have been angry, crying, hopeful. I have invited her to dinner. But nothing works. She feels sorry for me. That is the worst feeling.

I cry. I admit it. I've talked to some friends. I also have a male cousin who is gay and I talk with him the most.

I've driven by her home. I suppose I'm trying to find out something. But it makes me feel depressed.

We have mutual friends and I try to act like it doesn't bother me but it really does so I don't ask about her.

I haven't felt suicidal but I am depressed. I'm tired a lot and I also have trouble sleeping. Every time I wake up, for a few seconds I don't realize that I'm depressed but every day it sinks in and it's like I've been dumped all over again.

I don't know if she's seeing anyone else. I really don't want to know. When I looked on her Facebook page, I was looking to see about that. She gave no indication. I think if I found out she was with another guy, I would be devastated.

> *Where you used to be, there is a hole in the world, which I find myself constantly walking around in the daytime, and falling in at night. I miss you like hell.*
>
> *Edna St. Vincent Millay*
> *quotegarden.com*

A short time ago I did see a psychic. She told me my ex might reconsider in six to eight months. She said that she saw me with another woman and that I would be married in three years but I don't know that I believe it. I have called the psychic a couple of times. She tells me the same thing. I ask her if there is anything I can do but she says no, I need to be patient.

I wish there was a way to say something and make her see me differently. I think about that all the time. What can I do or say? Why did she stop loving me? How can I make her want me again? These thoughts swim in my head all the time. I have not come up with anything. It hurts and I hate it.

I would like to get married to my ex. It doesn't look like I'll get my wish. I'm going to have to find a way to get over this. I hate feeling this way. It makes me feel like a loser and lonely.

I went on a date a few weeks ago. It was okay. It was nice enough but it hasn't made me miss my ex girlfriend any less. If a woman came along whom I really liked, I would try a relationship. I can't say I'm looking for one. All I can think about is my ex.

I would like to meet someone new who I could get excited about. That feels so far away from me.

43 Straight

When I was thirty-one, I met the love of my life at a party. She was a tall leggy brunette and got my attention immediately. It was love at first sight. A friend introduced us and from that moment on, I knew she was the one. It was just an overwhelming feeling and something new to me. Prior to meeting her, I had some relationships, slept with some women but I had never felt anything like this. We used to talk about this special "thing" between us. We felt lucky and we were together all the time.

After we had been together a year, we decided to get married. Her family had money and offered to pay for the wedding. I had little to do with the planning and she loved every minute of it.

The wedding was to take place a year after we announced our engagement. I was thrilled. Some of my buddies made jokes about only having sex with her for the rest of my life and never feeling the rush of a new person. But I figured that we would just always find a way to keep things fresh and new.

About three months before the big day, she told me she got a call from her ex and he wanted to see her. She explained that she had no feelings for him but was concerned because he recently lost his mother. I told her I was fine with it but secretly I didn't want her to meet him.

From then on, right up to the day of the wedding, she seemed preoccupied and I grew a little nervous. I asked her what was going on and she would always tell me everything was fine and that she was just anxious about all the wedding plans. I chose to believe her.

Our wedding day arrived and everything was set for a beautiful ceremony. It was very elegant and understated. One hundred fifty people were invited and everyone came. But she never did. It was fucking awful. First we thought she was late. Then we thought something happened to her. No one could get hold of her. She just never showed.

I can't even begin to explain what was going through my mind. I was broken, humiliated, scared, confused. It took her a month to contact me. When she did, I was in a deep depression. She said she was sorry but she couldn't go through with it and she didn't know how to tell me at the time.

I was too depressed to be angry. I lost twenty pounds that month. I just sat there on the phone, listening as she gave her litany of excuses. I hung up on her.

About three months after I was left at the altar, I found out that she was with her ex. That was part of why I was so devastated. I couldn't understand how she could just blow me off like that. She is married to him and they have children. It used to hurt me but now I just feel pity for her. I think someone who could do that to another is a sad, shallow person.

The deep depression lasted a year. I lost my job; I was sick a lot and had to move back in with my parents. They made me seek counseling. I went to therapy for five years. It took me a good solid two years to get back to somewhat normal.

I never asked her to get back together. Even if the thought occurred to me, I was mentally incapacitated and never would have trusted her.

I cried, sobbed and stared at the wall for hours on end. I didn't eat and slept all the time: sixteen to seventeen hours a day. I watched TV and drank a lot and never really talked to anyone but my therapist about it. I cut myself off from all of my friends. When I had to move back in with my parents, no one even knew where I was and eventually, I heard that my friends thought I killed myself.

> **Love is like a puzzle. When you're in love, all the pieces fit but when your heart gets broken, it takes a while to get everything back together.**
>
> *Author Unknown*
> *quotegarden.com*

In therapy, I mostly talked and my therapist would listen. Sometimes I was given homework, like to list things in my life I wanted to accomplish. I went to counseling for five years and the last two were the most beneficial. I was finally starting to find myself again and that's when the real work began.

The most embarrassing thing to me is how I lost all sense of myself—that I allowed another person to make me so lost and miserable. I learned in therapy that what she did was horrible but what I *allowed* her to do to me was a waste of energy and life.

It took me a little over five LONG years to get over being jilted. While I was going through the depression, I replayed the good times we had over and over and over and would imagine she begged to get back with me. But I knew she wouldn't and she didn't. I didn't try to contact her or snoop around in her life.

I went on my first date three years after all of this happened. For the longest time, I swore I would never fall in love again. My confidence was destroyed. That first date was awkward and there was no second date. It was too painful for me. I went through the motions but I didn't have any fun.

It was four years before I had sex again. I know, I know. I barely even masturbated. I had little drive for life because of what she did to me. When I finally did have sex, it was with a woman I had been seeing for about two months. We are still together and I love her.

I have nothing to say to my ex. I still hold some resentment but mostly I try to concentrate on the positive and appreciate that I am now in a happy relationship. I believe in soul mates and think we can have more than one. I feel as though I've met mine but after what happened, I'm not sure if I want to get married. If I ever do, it will be a quick ceremony at the courthouse. I don't think I could handle anything more.

40 Straight

I found out my wife was having an affair. We were married for ten years and have one child. I got an anonymous email alerting me to the fact she was carrying on with a coworker and that I should be aware. When I got the email, I was stunned and wasn't sure if it was true. At first I was going to confront her but the more I thought about it, I figured if it was true, she would most likely deny it.

She often had "girls night" so I figured I would follow her. On the night she was going out, I said I was going out too. I borrowed a friend's car and waited by our home until she left. I followed her to a restaurant. She went in and I followed shortly after. Sure enough, she met him. They hugged and kissed and it wasn't platonic. I walked up to her and told her the marriage was over and left. She followed me out trying to talk to me. I got in my car and sped off.

I was filled with rage. She lied to me. For how long? I was driving recklessly and I'm glad I got my friend his car back in one piece. But I was destroyed. I literally didn't know how to be me anymore. Everything changed.

I thought our marriage was good. I still loved her. I needed to get out of that house but our son made it difficult. I couldn't leave him but I couldn't stay. When she and I finally spoke, she told me it was nothing, just attention. She tried to make out like I didn't fulfill her needs and that was the only reason she turned to someone else. She said she didn't love him and she wanted to make it work between us but I couldn't. SHE LIED to me. She would get dressed up and say she was meeting her girlfriends and kiss me goodbye while I stayed home with our son and she would go off and fuck this other guy. I wanted to stay married but I didn't trust her and I didn't like her anymore.

> **When truth is divided, errors multiply.**
>
> *Eli Siegel, Damned Welcome*
> *quotegarden.com*

For quite some time I was very sad, very devastated. I smoked pot, drank too much and felt very sorry for myself. All the while, I was going through divorce proceedings and a custody battle.

I tried to keep it together for my son. When I was with him, I was okay but he pleaded with me to get back with her. I couldn't tell him what happened. I tried to explain that we grew apart and it ripped my heart out.

I would talk with some of my divorced friends about it but I mostly concentrated on the divorce and custody part. No one wants to hear a man bellyache about a broken heart, at least not for very long.

I would try and remember every detail to see if she was justified in lying to me and cheating on me.

I cried for the first few months. I felt like a failure. I cried out of self-pity but also for my son. He would not have what I wanted for him. The divorce caused, and still causes him, stress and I feel that is my fault. It's more her fault but we are his parents and together we failed him.

I am over the hardest part of my divorce. I don't cry anymore but I still feel betrayed and hurt. I wish there was a way to make it right but I need to be strong for my son and see if I can make a new life for me and for him.

After about a year, I got back into the dating world. I was ready at that point, though I have a hard time trusting women now. Men usually get the bad reputation for cheating but women cheat. They are conniving and plotting. Eventually I met a woman with whom I started to feel more than just a physical attraction. We have been together now for seven months. I have explained to her what happened with my marriage. She told me she has been cheated on as well and we have been very open. I do care for her and hope to make it last. Since we both have similar fears, I am able to talk to her without feeling like I'm a wuss.

I'm not sure I will ever get over what my ex-wife did to me. I am the one who ended the marriage but it was only because of what she did. I had a very hard time and blamed myself for a long time. Her words echoed in my head about how the affair was my fault.

I would never get back with her. I don't think she is a horrible person but I will never feel desire for her again.

There is nothing I could say to my ex wife that would make a difference. She did what she did. She cheated. When you marry someone, you take vows and promise to be faithful. She broke those vows and it not only hurt me and our marriage but it hurt our son. He is the innocent. Her actions are going to play a part in who he is and for that I am angry with her. I wish I knew how not to be angry any more. I hope time helps.

THE OBSERVATION DECK

Psychic

Michelle
www.Madea-Michelle.com
15 years experience

In my experience the pain and shock associated with heartbreak are about the same in the beginning of the breakup, whether it is a man or a woman. The intensity of emotion is weighted by how much the individual invested in the relationship.

Healing is where there is a real difference. Women in our society are taught that they are free to express feelings, so they are more vocal about the pain they are going through. Verbal expression of emotion is a form of emotional healing. So is being comforted by our support group, which goes hand in hand with the expression of emotion. In our society we have more patience for women going through this for an extended period than we do for men. A woman can cry and express her pain for months with her girlfriends.

Our society teaches men "Big boys do not cry." And that ideal is reinforced constantly over their lives, both socially and in the media. Men do not have the same outlet of verbal expression and because of this, they don't get the same support a woman does. These two important forms of emotional healing are not available to men nearly as much as they are to women.

This is such a strong social norm that even if a man's parents go out of their way to teach him it's okay to express himself, there is a good chance his peers will teach him differently by the third grade. Boys who are emotional in the schoolyard tend to be singled out and bullied. So this social programming can be reinforced with violence at an early age. That's some pretty strong programming.

Saying "Ouch, this hurts!" is normal for women. We are very lucky to have this freedom. Men are taught to "suck it up."

Nor do men have the same type of support network women do. Women have other women to talk to. As a society, it is the social norm for a woman to be comfortable talking about the feelings she is having over a breakup for months or even longer. Men don't talk to each other about feelings nearly as much as women.

There is a beauty to the silent support I have seen tight groups of men give to each other during a break up. For each male friend a man has, there is usually one question his friend will ask him. It is a close-ended question: "Are you OK, Man?" The answer is always "I'm fine." Guys will be there for him but they will not expect him to discuss his feelings. Women would get very, very worried about another woman who will not talk about it. Men will assume another guy will talk about it if he wants to. At the same time, remember that third grade bullying? It has a strong impact. His buddies may support him silently and he may keep that silence. From that point on, the support group of the male will take him in the direction of "getting over her"—spending time with him, taking him out. This will only work if the man is ready to let go of the relationship. If not, he may go on with his life, even getting involved with other women while still silently aching for the one who broke his heart. Women are much more likely to wait. This is a lot easier to do when you can talk it out.

It makes things very difficult for men, who by society's standards, have to carry a poker face, even when in great pain. After a while, painful emotions get built up until the dam is ready to overflow. A man can carry pain around with him for years, until it literally erupts, usually in the form of an outburst of anger. This can be triggered by something as simple as a bolt that will not unscrew two years later.

When men call me for readings, it's almost always about heartbreak. I have women who come to me once or twice a year for a reading. I only have one male client who does that. Women feel it's all right to ask for help. Men are more likely to plan things on their own, or not plan at all and just take it as it comes. Men have the ability to focus on one thing at a time (this goes back to when men hunted for food. If they did not have complete focus, they could loose the game or their lives). Women generally think about multiple things at any given time (multi-tasking is a requirement of motherhood), tend to plan more and are used to having a verbal support network.

Both sexes are obsessive if they are not ready to let go of the relationship, however the questions are very different. Men want to know "How can I fix this?" Or "How do I make it work?" Men are very action oriented. Women want to know "When will he call?" The actions taken are also very different. Men are much more likely to try to fix things. Women are much more likely to wait and see how valuable they are to the man in question. This value is measured by the expression of feelings, i.e.: "When he calls."

Men *seem* to take it much better than women when I can't see an outcome they desire. Men are very polite about it and almost always say thank you. And then they hang up. The exception to this is if the emotional dam is about to overflow. If they have been trying for months to make a relationship work and there is an eventual breakup which cannot be fixed, they may lose it when I give them the news but this is very, very uncommon. I think I have had that happen twice in fifteen years. Women almost always express unhappiness and want to know why. This is where healing starts.

I have male clients who call over and over about the same issue but I don't encourage it. Going out and doing things is much more healing for the mind, heart and ego. The ratio is the same for women and men.

27 Straight

I met a woman at work. She and I work in different departments. She is incredibly beautiful: tall, raven hair, smart, sexy, she is all of it. I always thought she was out of my league. She is about an inch taller than I am and really a knockout. I'm not ugly but I think I'm average looking.

One night, we were at a party one of our coworkers threw. We wound up deep in conversation for a long time. As the night drew to a close, I walked her to her car. She asked me if I was ever going to ask her on a date. This was a huge surprise to me. I was so shocked and excited that I could barely form words. I managed to tell her that I would love to go out with her and we made plans to have dinner the following evening. Then we kissed. My stomach did flip-flops. I seriously could not believe this was happening to me but I was very happy about it.

Over the course of three months, we continued to see each other. I was in HEAVEN! She was MY girlfriend. My guy friends were in awe. I was on top of the world. I thought I did a pretty good job of remaining cool to her. I tried to not look overly anxious or grateful even though inside I was. Eventually I started to feel comfortable, to trust that we really had something real. I told her I was falling in love with her.

I could see in her eyes that my declaration of love freaked her out and I immediately regretted telling her. I felt sick to my stomach because I could just feel her pulling away. She didn't say it back and she left.

> *Love is like quicksilver in the hand. Leave the fingers open and it stays. Clutch it, and it darts away.*
>
> Dorothy Parker
> famousquotesandauthors.com

The next day at work, on a break, she told me she didn't feel the same for me and she wanted things to stop. I tried to tell her she didn't have to tell me she loved me, that nothing had really changed but she just said she felt it best we cool it - HER words.

I was so upset. I had to go back to work and act fine but I had zero concentration. I wanted to cry. I wanted to write her a letter, something, anything! When I got into my car, I started to cry. The reality really hit me and then I sobbed. I sobbed like a four year old missing his mommy. WTF??? How was I supposed to just go on now? One minute I am the luckiest guy in the world, the next I am dumped and alone.

The breakup was so hard because it came out of the blue. I thought we were TOGETHER. I got COMFORTABLE! She ruined my world. I hate that the way I feel has anything to do with her. I want so much to get back together with her. It's ALL I think about.

I sobbed, I drank, I sat alone all day on the weekend. I actually did call a psychic. She told me that this woman was moving on and that she started seeing another guy. I was told that I should start dating again and that I will meet someone within a year. This pissed me off and it's the last time I will ever call a psychic.

I have tried a few times to win her back. I have written her letters where I poured my soul out to her. I told her that I have never loved anyone before and I know if she would just give it a chance (we could make it work) but she hasn't.

It has been six months and I haven't dated anyone. I WISH I could go find someone just to have sex with. But I can't even think about being with anyone. I still want her back.

I am not over her. I found out that she is seeing someone. I asked her about it and she confirmed it. SHE ACTUALLY HAD THE AUDACITY to ask my advice. She told me she wants to be my friend and then ASKED ME for ADVICE about HIM! I told her she was on her own. The fact that she did that should be enough for me to call her a bitch and be done with her but I can't and it makes me feel stupid.

I've Googled her name and I do ask questions at work but I try to act like I'm not that curious. I've gone to her Facebook page and looked at her pictures and tortured myself. I wish I couldn't see it but I do look almost every day.

I think the most embarrassing thing is how pathetic I am. I want her and she doesn't care about me. I am not suicidal but I do feel desperate. WORST feeling ever! I feel awful. I am consumed with envy and don't understand what he has that I don't. I do know he's a really tall guy and that makes me wonder. I cannot compete with a tall guy. But I did think we had more than that. I guess not.

Do I believe in soul mates? NO!

In closing, I just want to say this: I get it, women. You can change your mind. But you don't have to rub it in our face, ask us advice on your new guy. Men are supposed to be macho and immune to "feelings" but we're not. We fall in love and we get hurt. Women can be very cold. I guess I am really angry now. At her, at me, at everything. I do hope the psychic is right and I will meet someone this year. I need a break!

44 Straight

My brother and his wife lived across the street from Melanie. One day we were all sitting on the porch and Melanie came outside. I saw her and said to my brother "One day I'm going to marry her." About a year later I did marry her. We were together for nineteen years and have two children.

About seventeen years into the marriage, I noticed a problem starting. I was getting too involved with my work, was spending sixteen hours a day working and I noticed she was becoming distant. I knew she wasn't feeling happy and felt like she wasn't getting enough attention. She had brought it up several times but I didn't pay that much attention to it. We went on several trips together but it just wasn't the same closeness.

I started wondering about my neighbor and thought she might be messing around with him because she started spending a lot of time with him. I started catching her hanging out over there when I was gone. I would come home and she would be with him. He was a friend of mine. Then I found out she had gotten him a job where she worked and that really made me start thinking. The entire time, whenever I would ask her about him, she would say, "You're crazy. It's all in your head. There's nothing going on." For a long time I believed her.

Another year went by and I started thinking she was messing around with this other guy. She denied it. I actually went through her emails and saw that she had typed "I love you." to him. When I confronted her, she said she wrote it as a friend. She convinced me I was totally insane and crazy for believing that, so I totally believed her.

Six months later my cousin called me to ask if his son, who was battling drugs, could stay with us. The rehab place was much closer to where I lived, so I agreed as long as he went to work and his classes. Melanie started taking him to these classes. They started spending a lot of time together. I never suspected them at all. I always suspected my neighbor and that other guy I know.

I had plans with my son to go fishing. We had a large home and my son slept with me that night so we wouldn't wake anybody up. We got up, got our stuff ready to go and I noticed my cousin's son had fallen asleep on the couch and Melanie had fallen asleep on the other couch.

About a half hour into the drive, I realized I forgot my fishing license so I came back. I hadn't locked the door. We jumped out of the truck and I left it running, so you couldn't even hear that we got out. We walked in and saw her on the couch with her legs spread open and he was nailing her.

> **About 24% of men and 14% of women have had sex outside their marriages, according to a Dec. 21, 1998 report in USA Today on a national study by the University of California, San Francisco.**
>
> *infidelityassistance.com*

I lost it. I was chasing the guy around the house and she started attacking me. He grabbed the keys and took her cell phone and our van that she used and took off. I was really mad. I broke our wedding picture, all kinds of stuff. The normal anger after you witness something like that. She called the police, so I packed up my clothes and my son's clothes and left. My son was totally mortified. However my seven-year-old daughter stayed behind.

We moved in with my brother a few states away. We were there for about one month when my wife called to tell me she was incapable of taking care of our daughter. There was too much going on and my cousin's son was too young to be around kids. So I drove back, straight through, picked up my daughter, was only there for literally thirty minutes and drove straight back.

When I saw my daughter, I could immediately see that she was undernourished. She only had one outfit.

Melanie had taken our entire life savings, twenty thousand dollars, the day before I left her. I had a secret account with sixteen hundred dollars and I used that to move.

At first I was a completely horrible father because I worked all day and left my son to watch my daughter at night. I was feeling bad so I would always go out. I would sleep with different women, at least thirty in two years. It was about a month after my separation before I started sleeping with other women. It really didn't make me feel any better. I was angry and was actually hurting these women intentionally. I wasn't trying to have a relationship with any of them. It wasn't that I was getting into relationships with them and then breaking their hearts. I would hang out with them for a few days and have one-night stands and then not call them back. There was one woman who I really did like. She had also been cheated on—her ex husband was living with the girl—and we both had daughters who were the same age, so we had a lot in common.

I was heartbroken over what had happened in my marriage. I couldn't believe she would do that to me. The worst part is how she made me feel crazy for two years, telling me that it was all in my head, like I was losing my mind. That and the fact that she had lied to my face were devastating.

The only reason I left was because I was so angry I thought I might kill her. I moved out of state to avoid that.

I never cried. I was so angry that I couldn't think of crying. I kept my feelings in. I did talk to my brother in depth about it one night. We discussed the circumstances, not how I felt, but he knew what I was going through because of the way I acted. I didn't really care about anything. In one year I lost fifty pounds. I wasn't eating, maybe one meal every couple of days.

I take responsibility for my part of what happened because she was showing signs that she needed more attention. When we married, she was a virgin, straight out of high school. She had never been with another man. That was the hugest mistake. She needed to experience other people before she got married.

It took me three years to get over her. I never wanted or tried to get her back. I would never forgive what she did, the betrayal. The reason I know I'm over her is because now, we live very close to each other and we talk because of the kids. I found out she had been sleeping with several men while we were married including lots of my friends and it didn't bother me. I was shocked but not upset.

I do believe in soul mates but I think it's pretty rare, but I do think you can have more than one.

When people become complacent in their relationship and start to take each other for granted, that's where you have a problem. You have to keep things fresh like when you first met. That's the biggest problem people have.

66 Straight

I've gone through two breakups that were hard for me. The first was the most difficult, maybe because it was the first. We'd been together for about three months. She thought I was getting too serious. She wanted to date others and told me that we should see other people. It was devastating and I never want to go through that ever again.

I never tried to get her back, as I thought it was pretty final. I felt a pain deep down inside of me but I didn't want to talk to anyone about it. I remember shedding some tears. I thought I was in love and felt my heart was breaking but it was a personal hurt. I kept it to myself and didn't talk it out with anyone. I didn't know what to do to make the hurt stop. Occasionally I would tell my mom about things that were happening but mostly I kept things to myself. I didn't know what to say and didn't want people to know that girl had broken my heart. I was afraid of being laughed at or made fun of.

I wasn't looking for another relationship. Things happen or they don't. I did have small infatuations with a few other girls but nothing serious. I've never jumped from bed to bed. Now days it happens a lot but not back in the 1960's. Not that I had been scarred by that girl but "once burned twice shy." I wasn't eager to start another relationship, sexual or otherwise. I didn't have a sexual relationship with her and I didn't have sexual relationships with any other girls. In fact, I wasn't intimate with anyone before I finally married in 1973. I didn't engage in meaningless sex. To me the sexual event is the high place of a relationship, to enhance it, to make the relationship better, not just to use girls to satisfy my own urges.

It took me several months before I began seeing another girl. But before too long, she and her family moved to another state. I took that loss much better.

I had a relationship with another girl just before I was drafted into the Army. It lasted for about six months. We did have a few intimate moments but there was no penetration, just kissing and fondling. It was hard to leave and it took a while to get over her too. At first, when I had to leave her, I was distraught and considered killing myself but realized I couldn't do that. I felt that was not the way and that it would be wrong to take my own life. I thought I loved her and I think she loved me too because she was waiting for me when I got out of the military two years later. We corresponded while I was away and when I got out I could have started seeing her again but I didn't pursue her. I often wonder what might have been with her but guess I will never know. I don't think she and I were meant to be.

I'm embarrassed about being naked with her before I went into the military. I shouldn't have taken advantage of her that way. She got pregnant and married someone a few years after I got out of the Army. Actually I was glad that she found someone. I felt guilty that I may have taken her to places she had never been before and may have contributed to her getting pregnant.

As far as getting over each of those girls, I learned to let things go and not to dwell on them or feel guilty about them. What happened just happened and maybe it was meant to be that way. Who says it was up to me? Things happen. Life happens.

Truly, I don't think I ever fell really hard for anyone. I had a few "loves"; at least they felt that way from my side. When I was in the military I was lonely and lost and wanted out while that girl was on my mind but I got involved in my life overseas, did what I was told to do and tried to do the best job I could do and I eventually got over her too.

I never felt the need for therapy or to seek advice from anyone. I just got involved in other things and eventually the girls faded from my mind.

I believe each of us has a "special someone" who we are meant to be with and in 1973, I met my special girl. We married and have had two kids! I don't think any of us has two soul mates, just the one and I can't even imagine NOT being married to mine.

That first girl, the one who broke my heart, still has a special place in my heart but she doesn't compare with my True Love, the woman I have now and have been with for thirty-seven years.

> *Soul mates are people who bring out the best in you. They are not perfect but are always perfect for you.*
>
> *Author Unknown*
> *quotegarden.com*

24 Straight

My girlfriend left me three months ago. We met two years ago at a party my best friend threw for me. There were about a hundred people there and Susan came in with her friends. I thought she was cute but I was kind of into another girl at the time. As the night went on, one of her friends came up to me and told me Susan wanted to make out with me but she said I had to pretend that I didn't know this. I figured "Fuck it! Free bootie!" So I found my way over to her and struck up a conversation. She was already pretty drunk and was totally flirting with me.

She was kind of being a little slutty but I was turned on. After about fifteen minutes, we hooked up in a bedroom and made out for a long time. We didn't have sex even though I tried. She kept saying she was a good girl and then laughed really hard. Eventually her friends found us and told her it was time to go. They had to pull her off of me.

I must admit I felt a little like a rock star. I never got her last name or number or anything. I thought about her all the time after that and wanted to know how to find her. A few days later, she friended me on Facebook. I played it real cool but I was totally psyched that she found ME! She would send me messages and we chatted for a while. I casually asked her on a date and she said yes.

On the way to pick her up, I started getting butterflies in my gut and this freaked me out. I had never felt nervous for a date before. She opened the door and that was it for me. I swear it was love at second sight. I knew I had to play it off like I was chill and I should win an Oscar for that!

We just had a good thing going. We were together all the time. I bought her all kinds of stuff like a sound system for her car, a ring, a flat screen. She never felt like it was enough and always told me I needed to make more money if I ever even wanted to think about marrying her. I got a better job, I tried to be the guy she wanted me to but it was never enough. I started acting like a damn dog. If she told me to do something, I did it. My friends all said I was whipped and I guess I knew I was but I couldn't seem to help it. I was in love with her and I wanted her to be happy.

Three months ago, she told me that she wanted to break it off. This was totally out of the blue. I didn't see it coming. I freaked on her, started crying. I begged her to reconsider. She was so fucking cold! Just no emotion at all. She said she didn't love me anymore and that I needed to give her space. It was so hard for me because I LOVED HER!!!!! I did everything for her and she just used me.

I tried over and over again to get back with her. I called, sent flowers and I even tried to get her by telling her I would spoil her more. That makes me cringe. OH! I was a damn fool for her. She never replied to any emails, she blocked me from Facebook (all her friends did too).

I was fucking miserable. I have cried and even thrown temper tantrums when I am alone. I talk to her out loud. My friends would think I am a total fag. I hate her but I miss her and I keep trying to figure out what I can do. Nothing works. I have told some friends that I miss her but NO ONE knows how I really feel. I feel desperate and totally alone like I am never going to find anyone like her again. I hope and pray that she decides to give me another chance because I would do anything for her.

I have not dated anyone. I hooked up with one girl at a party and we had sex but it made me feel worse. I could only think of my ex the whole time and afterward I went home and cried.

I admit I've called her and then hung up. I've driven by her house too but have stopped doing that. I've done everything: Googled her name, tried to find out things through mutual friends, tracked her through social media. I even created a fake Facebook to see if she would friend me but she didn't.

> ***Desperation is like stealing from the Mafia: you stand a good chance of attracting the wrong attention.***
>
> *Douglas Horton*
> *brainyquote..com*

Everything about this is embarrassing. I can't tell anyone how sad I am. No one would understand. They would call me weak or tell me to go date other people but I don't want anyone else. I wish every minute of every day that we'll get back together. I keep hoping she'll change her mind.

I do feel desperate but not so much suicidal. I often wish I was dead but I feel like that would be the day she would want me back. I think she is seeing someone but I haven't found out for sure.

If she were standing here in front of me, I would tell her how much I love her and that no one will EVER love her the way I do. I would do anything for her. I want to have children with her. I want to take care of her. I believe in soul mates and she is mine. I want to marry her. Sometimes I think if I just want it bad enough, it'll happen but other times I feel so stupid.

53 Straight

When I was in high school, I dated Jean. We were together for our entire senior year. It was a very typical high school relationship. We loved each other. She lost her virginity to me. We made plans to marry and have kids. I was accepted into a college in another state. We figured we'd see each other on breaks. She applied too and we hoped that she would eventually transfer to my school.

After I left for school, we kept up a long distance relationship for a while but life intervened. Eventually we grew apart and never realized the hopes and dreams we had of making a life together. Neither one of us was devastated. We both became involved with other people and lost touch.

Several years after college, I got married. We tried to conceive but after arduous testing, it became clear my wife was unable to bear children. This put a lot of stress on our marriage, though we did make a great effort. Eventually the effort was just not enough. We lost the love we once had and decided to divorce. It was quite amicable. There were no hard feelings. I did feel sad that we were unable to make it last. I believe she felt the same but the love was gone and we saw no reason to stay in a loveless marriage.

As I was getting used to single life again, Jean found me through some mutual high school friends. I was excited. I had such fond memories of her. We decided to meet for lunch.

When I laid eyes on her, my heart skipped a beat. I knew she was my woman. I just knew it. Later, she admitted she felt the same way but made an effort to look cool. We would laugh at that many times.

We got together and stayed together. We were together for almost six years and I was the happiest I had ever been.

I noticed over a period of time that Jean suffered severe mood swings. I urged her to seek medical attention, therapy but she didn't—or wouldn't. She never did and I can't point to a particular diagnosis of her behavior. I will say it did not seem like bipolar. There were long periods of time when she was fine. But then she would get hit with severe lethargy, depression and would cry and cry. She would pull away from me and cut me out while she went through this dark period. Over the course of five years the depression would come on more frequently and last longer, one time for two months.

This tore me up. I loved her so much and seeing her like this made me feel powerless. Men like to fix problems and I had no idea what to do. She completely resisted any suggestion of therapy and maintained she could handle it. She told me that if I really loved her, I would accept this about her and not push. So I didn't push.

Writing this is quite difficult for me. The last time she went through one of these depressed states, she was darker than I had ever seen her. It was on my mind when I went to work that day. I decided that, despite her resistance, I would somehow force her to get medical attention for her intense depression. Once I made the decision, I felt empowered. I finally found some control and I had hope that we would get her to a place where she could lead a fairly normal life. I researched doctors and started to formulate a plan of action.

When I arrived home, the house was dark. I knew she'd been in bed all day and probably hadn't had anything to eat or drink. I went to the kitchen and got her some water. I went into the bedroom. As I suspected, she was in bed. I sat down and nudged her to wake her up. She lay there cold. My heart sank. I looked on the nightstand and saw an empty bottle of sleeping pills. The prescription noted there were thirty pills. There were none that I could find. I don't know how many she took but she took enough to end her life.

She left no note. This all happened over a decade ago and remembering the details is still very painful for me. Most of the time I can stuff it down but it does get to me from time to time. I often blame myself. If I would have come to the decision earlier about making her get help, she might still be here. She was sick and I allowed her illness to dictate my lack of action.

Initially I was numb. I couldn't cry for a very long time. I was sad but I didn't know how to release the pain. I wanted to cry but it took more than a year for me to do so. When I did, I cried every day for a month.

I have dated a few times but am not comfortable with the idea of getting too close to anyone. It seems the relationships I've been in have failed. The breakup of my marriage was not devastating but to me it felt like failure. Maybe one day I will meet a woman who will convince me to risk it but she has not introduced herself to me yet.

I don't remember exactly how long it was before I had sex but it was years. On one hand, I enjoyed the physical release but on the other, it was difficult not to think of Jean. There have been a handful of times since her death that I have had sex but I mostly choose not to because it brings back painful memories.

Jean perished over twelve years ago. I am over the hardest part. It isn't fresh anymore but the pain lingers. I still blame myself at times and occasionally I have a full-fledged breakdown.

I think about her every day. I wish I could have helped her sooner. It eats at me.

I attended grief counseling in the months after her death. It was group counseling for those who lost someone to suicide. We discussed our feelings and helped each other. At the time it was imperative that I attend those sessions. It helped me to keep sane and kept me from being overcome with self-blame. I was not able to stay friends with any of the nice people in that group. I wanted to extricate myself from the negative feelings associated with Jean's passing, so eventually I stopped going and tried to put my life into a place that had no reminders. Funny though, the more you try to run from reminders, the more aggressive they become. So I realized that I should accept whatever happens. If I am reminded of her, I acknowledge it and try my best to move on.

> *The current economic cost of depressive illness is estimated to be 30-44 billion dollars a year in the United States alone. In addition to considerable pain and suffering that interfere with individual functioning, depression affects those who care about the ill person, sometimes destroying family relationships or work dynamics between the patient and others. Therefore, the human cost in suffering cannot be overestimated.*
>
> emedicine.medscape.com/article/805459-overview

THE OBSERVATION DECK

Bartender

Bob

I have seen relationships break up and the after results, at least in the bar scene, are almost always the same with only a few exceptions. Group A: They just get drunk and try to get laid. Group B: Spend hours on the phone trying to fix it and/or get into fights.

Sometimes, if they get drunk enough, they'll look to others in the bar to see if they were in the wrong or find reasons why it wasn't their fault. I've been told by more than one in a slurred voice, "You're lucky you don't have to deal with this kind of crap." But there are a few who have asked my opinion on the matter. They'll drink, brag, drink some more, fight, drink some more and then try to get laid. As far as becoming more vocal after they've had too much to drink, pretty much everyone who drinks a bit too much becomes vocal, hostile to some point and defensive.

There was one couple who broke up and the guy wanted to beat the crap out of her father, who was also in the bar, because he felt that her father was part of the reason.

I was working a wedding reception and the groom and the father-in-law were doing shots at the bar. All of a sudden the bride came out from the hall up to her new husband and proceeded to give him a solid right hook, dropping him to the floor, followed by the bridesmaids who began to kick and spit on him. The reception only lasted for an hour. They had four hundred guests with a dinner service. The bride found out the night before that the groom slept with one of the bridesmaid's sisters the night of his stag party.

We used to do a 4th of July event (very large, 45,000 people a day through the place), so when I was not bartending I would help with security. I was with one other guy helping with security as we walked up to this 5'3" skinny as hell girl who just hauled off and slugged her boyfriend in the gut with a full, pissed off swing. This guy was about 6'4" and skinny too and saw us standing there and he had this look of "What am I supposed to do?" The girl turned around and saw us and said, "I didn't do anything." We had to escort her off the property.

Generally, with my regular crowd, I don't see a lot of people trying to ease the pain of a breakup by trying to hop into bed with someone.

This may sound a bit weird, but it is not just a worst case as a single event. I've had several couples who were happily married for a long time and when one became ill and passed away, the other seemed to follow within six months. The one that hit home for me was when we found out that this woman was terminal and it spread real fast (cancer); they gave her a couple of months to live. She tried radiation and after a short period she could no longer deal with it. She came to the bar to say her goodbyes to everyone and went home to die. Her husband fell into a deep, deep depression but slowed his drinking. He passed away four weeks later from a heart attack. Watching someone that ill come to say goodbye was real hard.

I guess that there are different types of heartbreaks ranging from relationship breakup, death or just an illness. Outside the bar it seems to be a different scene but most people in the bar are just trying to get drunk, get laid or drink until they no longer hurt. Coming from a personal experience, I drank HARD for years to try to forget.

What I see the most is who is cheating on whom and seeing the poor kids who have to sit there while the parents get loaded and fight.

57 Straight

I was with Meredith for a total of seven years. We were both divorced. I have two children from another marriage. Meredith had no children. We moved in together in the fourth year of our relationship.

She was the easiest woman to be with. We rarely had a disagreement and when we did, we would work it out and get over it quickly. She gave me my space. She never put pressure on me and vice versa. We fit and it felt really good. Above all, we were always truthful with each other.

In the last year of our relationship, I was on a business trip and I had sex with a woman whom I didn't know. To be honest, I don't even remember her name. I had been drinking. I met her in the bar. She was attractive and really coming on to me. I don't know why I gave in. I had been on many trips without Meredith and other attractive women had made sure to let me know they were willing and interested and though it was tempting, I resisted. I was with Meredith and I loved her. I had always been faithful to her but on this particular evening I gave in. I felt guilty the morning after, I really did, but I decided it was best to think of it as a one-time thing. I figured it best not to tell her. She would be so upset and it really was meaningless to me. I was pretty drunk and I honestly don't remember most of it.

When I returned home, Meredith picked me up from the airport and I remember feeling very guilty looking at her smiling face. Two nights prior, I had cheated on her. Here she was, rush hour traffic, insisting on picking me up instead of me taking a shuttle. She brought food and snacks. This made me feel like a real jerk. I tried to not think about it.

About two weeks later, I started to notice that I was itching. I literally thought I got jock itch: until Meredith started complaining that she was also itching. When she brought this up to me, I knew what it meant. I needed to come clean and that it would hurt her. I looked like a sleaze bag bringing home a nasty case of crabs to the woman who was always truthful and faithful to me.

For a brief moment I thought about making something up. Saying it could be the hotel but I knew she wouldn't buy it so I told her everything. She just sat there. Her face held no expression. She listened to me and after I finished she seemed disappointed and told me she needed to go to her mother's house to think. I wanted to argue with her but I knew I needed to let her process what I had just said.

> **Crabs (pubic lice) are small parasites that feed on human blood. They can be sexually transmitted even if there is no penetration or bodily fluid exchanged or even if a condom is worn. They can live 24 hours off a human host, making it possible to get crabs from infested bedding or clothes. Animals do not get crabs.**
>
> *randomhistory.com*

She was gone for three days. We had no contact. I missed her so much and felt terrible. I told my best friend. He thought that maybe after she thought about it, realized that I had never cheated on her before and was really drunk, that she could live with it. I might have to really work hard for her for a year but she wouldn't let some stupid one-night stand ruin a good relationship.

It was a Saturday when she walked through the door. She told me she had some things to say to me. She told me that she had made compromises to be with me. Some that I had no idea about and then she proceeded to tell me of a man who worked very hard for her affections during the first two years of our relationship. A short time after we'd met, she had met another man. She dated both of us. He was very successful and he was a good man. At this time, she had not had sex with either one of us. When it came time for her to choose, she explained she based her decision on love and trust. She said something inside of her knew I would be the best choice for her because she knew she could really trust me. Ouch!

She also went on to tell me of other ways she sacrificed to make our relationship work. She was calm and somber. Then she announced that what I had done ruined that trust and she could no longer be with me. She didn't seem angry. Sometimes I wish she was and perhaps the outcome would have been different. She carried a huge weight and said she was sending some friends and family over to pack and move her things. She asked me to make sure to get everything of hers ready and available for them. She gathered some more of her personal belongings and asked me not to contact her.

I felt destroyed. I lost the woman I truly loved because my dick was hard for some one-night stand with crabs. I was and am humiliated. I've tried to fall back on the excuse that men cheat all the time but the truth is that I was really happy with Meredith and before this one incident, it was never difficult for me to remain faithful.

It has been five years since the day she left. After about a month, I started my quest to win her back. I begged, I pleaded. I assured her I would never do anything like this again. I offered to see a counselor. I sent flowers. I did everything I could think of but she eventually told me I needed to stop. For her, the relationship had been destroyed and even though she wanted to move past it, she could not. She asked me not to contact her anymore, that it was too painful for her, so I stopped.

She has not contacted me and I have done as she asked.

This has been a very difficult thing to accept. I still cannot believe I lost Meredith the way I did. I have never been able to justify it or not feel like a complete asshole. Sometimes I am upset that she couldn't find it in herself to forgive me. I try to put myself in her shoes and I honestly cannot say how I would feel. Would I forgive her?

There have been times in these five years that I have cried. I have been angry, lonely and very sad. I blame myself and there is nothing I can do to fix it.

I date. There are a few women I spend time with. I make no promises to them. Maybe I would if I fell in love. I'd really like to be in love and share my life with someone. I still wish Meredith would come back. I think of that every major holiday. New Year's Eve is especially hard for me. We always stayed in and played board games by the fire, made decadent dinners and had a really great time. Now I spend New Year's alone. I get invited to places but I always claim to be busy. It's almost like my punishment.

I hope that one day I can forgive myself. I also hope that either Meredith finds her way back to me or I find someone who I can love. The truth is I think I am going to be alone. I think I really blew it. There is a part of me that hopes she reads my story and comes home. Maybe she will. I think she was/is my soul mate.

41 Straight

I have had two significant breakup experiences in my life. It took me twenty years to get over my first love. The most recent occurred two months ago and I am still not okay about it. I have had crushes that I never got a chance with. I think a policy of no contact is best if it just can't happen because if you stick around, most will just take advantage of you. I have been that guy and they love it and will use you until you are dead.

I was with the most recent woman for six months. She, like the woman from twenty years ago, was just recently divorced. It was very hard because I listened to her words instead of paying attention to her actions. She told me everything I wanted to hear and in the end it turned out I was just being used as a rebound. After forty-one years of being single, I thought I had found the one for me. She used me up and smashed me. We broke up because she was done with me and wanted to be free again.

I actually tried to leave the relationship on many occasions but she always knew the right thing to say to get me back, such as, "Are you sure this is really what you want? Couldn't you just come over so we can talk about it?"

I have done everything to try and cry in order to get over this but cannot seem to cry at all. I have complained to friends, looked to horoscopes and signs, etc., even going so far as getting tarot readings. I have felt insane at times, seeing commercials that use her name or seeing things she likes pop up in posts on Facebook or on TV. I keep thinking these are signs that I should call her but I won't. I share my feelings with friends I can trust. Sometimes I honestly think my suffering is due to the fact that we sinned together and this is my correction from God. I really believed her when she said she wanted to be with me forever but it was all a lie to keep me around while she used me as a base to get strong after her marriage so she could feel confident enough to meet other men. She even kissed one of my friends and I forgave her.

I can't even think about dating at this point. Anyone else would just be a rebound and I would not do that to anyone. So I will wait it out until I am feeling healthy enough to date.

I have not had sex because I know it would only make my heart feel worse. I have been there and done that before. You cannot cure heartache with meaningless sex. That's a total illusion.

I secretly wish I could get her back but really I want the version of her I thought I was getting, which was probably all an act. Who knows? I do secretly want her back though.

> ***Tearless grief bleeds inwardly.***
>
> *Christian Nevell Bovee*
> quotegarden.com

There were times I would drive by her house but now I avoid driving down that road at all costs. I've Googled her name online, snooped around her life through mutual friends and looked up her photo on Facebook. It hurt and, in retrospect, was embarrassing. I don't recommend it.

I found out that she met someone else and it only served to show me that I was just a rebound. It was devastating to get that confirmation. I felt desperate and even thought about suicide.

I went to therapy over both women: this most recent and the woman from twenty years ago. It was the same therapist and she pointed out that each of these women were recently divorced and were nothing more than women who were very angry and looking for a rebound guy, even if they were not consciously aware of that fact. They lied, cheated and did anything they needed to do to keep me around until they got what they wanted. (In both cases, to do to a man all that their ex-husbands had done to them.) The awareness helps a little but the knowledge did not help to dull the pain. I wanted so much to believe that these two women had fallen for me as much as I fallen for them. Strangely enough, it wasn't until after their lies began that I fell for them. So it was really all an illusion. With each, I was planning on taking my time and they bumped up the speed with lies.

With both of these women, I can only hope that someone else will point out what they did to me, or that somehow God will through conviction. I know that nothing I can say would get through because people tend to ignore the reality of the hurt they cause and try to move on out of selfishness.

I used to believe in the concept of a soul mate but not any more. I really thought I'd found mine with the last woman. Despite it all, I would still like to spend the rest of my life with one person.

The biggest heartbreaks I have gone through were when I was down and vulnerable and allowed myself to get suckered into someone else's evil game. I would tell everyone to keep their eyes open to action and forget the words people say. Words are easy, especially for desperate liars. Only get into a relationship when you are feeling strong. People who want to use others can smell a potential victim from a mile away.

45 Confused

I am married with three children. My wife and I married young, in our early twenties. Looking back, I married her because I felt that was what I should do. We dated and had a lot in common. We both came from upper middle class families; both attended college (where we met) and graduated at the top of our class. We both had the same idea of the kind of lifestyle we wanted to create. At the time I felt happy. She is a good woman and a great mother.

She became friends with a woman many years ago who was also married. My wife invited the couple to dinner one weekend and I met the husband.

From the start he and I got along. He is a dynamic man. Very funny and, after a short period of time, he invited me to play golf. At first, nothing felt out of the ordinary to me. The more we hung out, the more I enjoyed his company. I started to prefer spending time with him. One night I dreamed that he and I were sexual and it was highly erotic. I woke from the dream very disturbed yet completely turned on. I was so bothered by this. How could this be? I am not gay. I have never fantasized about a man and never felt an attraction to one before. I told no one of my dream and tried to push it down. But the thought of the sex with him was almost too much for me. The desire only grew after that point. On the occasions when we played golf after the dream, I sensed a certain energy coming from him and I wondered if he felt the same.

> **20 percent of all gay men in America are in a heterosexual marriage.**
>
> marriage.about.com/cs/straightspouses/a/straightspouse.htm

On a day our wives took the kids out, I invited him over to help me do some work around the house. I will spare you the details of how it got started but within two hours we engaged in the most fulfilling and satisfying sex I had ever experienced. It was mind blowing. Immediately afterward, we felt awkward and he left. I swore to myself it would never happen again but before I knew it we started seeing each other regularly. We went to hotels, planned golf trips and I found myself developing feelings for him. I started to feel jealous if he spent time with other men and wondered if he did this with them. When I asked him about it, he told me that I was the only man he was with and wanted to be with.

This relationship went on for five and a half years. No one ever found out about us. I fell in love with him but I felt disgusted. I felt I was living a lie and didn't know what to do about it. He professed his love for me and we decided that we would just have to keep up the façade of our married lives because neither one of us knew how to explain this to any of our friends and family.

In the midst of our relationship, *Brokeback Mountain* came out. My wife, who is religious (I am not), had some pretty hateful things to say about the film and I remember feeling immense guilt. I watched the film alone when it went to video and it made me feel awful. I thought about the consequences of exposing my relationship and what it would do to everyone I loved. I was filled with anxiety about my double life so I decided to end the relationship with him.

We met and I told him we had to stop. It was awful. He begged me to continue the way we had been, that no one even suspected and he didn't know how to be happy without me. I couldn't do it anymore. It was breaking me. I felt love for him but I also felt what we were doing was wrong on so many levels. He tried for some time to get back to the way things were between us but I would not allow it. He tried to promise me that no one would ever have to know but these things have a way of getting out.

For the next couple of years things were very uncomfortable. We still all saw each other as couples. He would call me and try to get back together but I told him he needed to move on and to stop asking me. He wrote emails, he cried and it was all I could do to keep my sanity. Eventually he and his family moved about an hour away. This made it easier to stop seeing each other and slowly but surely, we stopped talking altogether. Our wives are still friends but I avoid seeing him.

I felt intense pain. I haven't cried. It's more like something inside of me has died. I feel numb about it. I have told NO ONE. It is something I will have to live with. I miss him all the time. I fantasize about living with him and sharing my life with him. It will never happen. I know sometimes I can be abrasive with my wife. I know it's because I secretly resent having to stay with her but it is the choice I made long ago and we have children. I must sacrifice my own desires so they can have a good life and feel they come from a respectable family.

The breakup was so hard for me because I felt like I was in love with him but I felt wrong. To this day, I do not define myself as a gay man. I broke up with him because I couldn't keep living a lie. The guilt was consuming me. I still feel consumed with guilt but at least I made the decision to stop it before any of our families got hurt.

I have not been with another man and I don't intend to. I do find myself wondering what it would feel like to be with another man, though. I wonder if I would fall in love with another man. I believe without a doubt I could enjoy sex with men but the feeling of love? I don't know. I will never find out.

It has been many years since we've seen each other. I can't say I'm completely over him. I think about him all the time and wish there was a way we could be together but there isn't, so that is how it has to be. Even though I loved him, I find the situation itself to be the most embarrassing thing that has ever happened to me.

To know me is to know I am not a dramatic man. I have felt desperate at times but more because I question my sexual identity. I did not expect this to be an issue I would have to deal with. I have always been matter of fact. I am not a "romantic." I would not take my own life for any reason. This relationship, though, has proved to be the most difficult experience of my life.

I don't know if he's been with anyone else and I don't want to know. Fortunately, I don't have to hear about anything he may be doing. I think if I did find out he was with another man I would be very upset about it.

I'm not over him but it's a goal I aspire to and I work on it daily. I have not sought therapy nor will I. I will deal with the consequences of my actions and do my best to conceal it from my family. I have said my piece to him but I do wish I could tell him I love him and feel I always will.

34 Straight

When I met my ex-girlfriend, she was pursuing a career that would put her in the public eye. We met four years ago at a Memorial Day party. I liked her a lot from the start. She is very pretty and a lot of men at the party were trying to get her attention. I was thrilled when I asked her to dinner and she said yes.

At that point, she hadn't reached success in her field. She was working and earning money but she was very focused on her main goal. I had my work but it is more pedestrian. I know I will never be rich but I make a good living and will continue to grow my business. Sometimes I wondered if she made it, if she would mind that I would not be making what she was aiming for. But I would put it out of my head.

We were together for a little over three years. The last year and a half of our relationship, she started to get the success she was after. She was making progress. She isn't a big name celebrity but she is well known locally. Once she caught a break her career took off very quickly. She traveled a lot and worked all the time. We spent less and less time together and it took a toll on our love life.

I started to secretly resent her career. I never complained. I hoped she would find success but it was interfering with our relationship.

There was a month when we didn't see each other at all. She was on the road. She would call and check in but she was very busy. When I called her, she rarely answered. We would email but we were growing apart and it was hurting me.

At the time, I felt sad and lonely. One of my friends invited me out and I met another woman who was all over me. It would have been easy to sleep with her and I considered it. I felt neglected and hadn't had sex for a long time. I didn't cheat on her though.

When she came home from her trip, she told me another trip was planned for the following week. She would be gone again for a month. I couldn't handle it. It took me a few days but I ended up telling her that I was lonely. I wanted more from her. She tried to explain that I knew what she had been working for when we met. She couldn't stop now. I understood that but it was too hard for me. She was moving on without me. People knew who she was. She was making tons of money. I felt like I wasn't enough. I was afraid that she would be on the road and meet some man who was more than I am or ever will be. I didn't tell her this but it was what I thought about. So I told her I couldn't be with her anymore. She was upset. She cried and told me she loved me but I didn't see myself waiting around for her while she was always traveling. We were living different kinds of lives.

It's been almost a year. It's really hard on me because she is a local public figure. She is on TV and talked about on the radio. It feels like I can't escape her. I know I'm the one who broke it off but it doesn't make it any easier. Sometimes I think I made the wrong choice. I have talked with my sister about it. My sister tells me that I should go with my heart but I am confused. If I got back together with her, I know it would eat at me. I would resent her success and feel inferior.

I can't stand knowing about her life. I hear about it from friends. They'll say, "Did you hear? Your ex is doing this or doing that." I've considered moving to another state but all my friends and family are here.

I have dated and I have had sex. It's something to do. I always like sex but I'm not in love with any of the women I've been with. I don't know if my ex is seeing anyone. I hope NOT to hear about it. But I keep dreading that one day, I'll find out.

I question my decision all the time. At this point, I'm not even sure if I called her and said I wanted her back, if she would be interested. We haven't talked since the breakup. She probably hates me.

Sometimes, when I drink too much, I cry. I listen to songs we used to listen to together and I just sit there and cry like a baby. I miss her and how it was before she found her success. I feel like an ass for how I am.

I just don't have an answer that satisfies me at all.

> **Yes, I will go. I would rather grieve over your absence than over you.**
>
> *Antonio Porchia, Voces, 1943*
> *translated from Spanish by W.S. Merwin*

39 Straight

I was married to Lynn for the better part of fourteen years. Both of us are creative people and have made our living in creative fields, which means money was/is sporadic. Sometimes we made a lot of money and then we had some slim years. We had a modest savings. Toward the last years of our marriage, my parents were helping us out financially. Because of this, they tried to dictate how we would live our lives. They tried to convince us to look into more secure work. It was hard to escape their lectures because they were helping us pay our rent. We both resisted this idea but Lynn would urge me to look into a "real job." She wasn't looking for one. She would say that because I am the man, I had to make sure to provide for the family. We don't have children because we don't have a steady, reliable source of income.

The pressure was mounting and our relationship suffered. I would battle with myself about giving up my dream of being creative for a living. We argued and it got pretty uncomfortable. As uncomfortable as it was, I always took my marriage vows seriously. "For better or for worse."

> **Oaths are but words, and words but wind.**
>
> *Samuel Butler*
> *quotegarden.com*

I was up for a big deal creative job, one that could have bought us some time and relief from asking my parents for help and getting them off of our backs. Lynn and I were both very hopeful about it but the deal fell through. I didn't lose it; it just never came to pass.

Soon after, Lynn announced to me that she wanted a divorce. I knew the reason. We were arguing a lot. Money was tight. She told me she wanted security—that when we got married, we were young and it was easy then to go with the flow. But now that we were getting older, she didn't feel comfortable staying in a marriage where all we did was fight and worry about money.

I tried to rationally talk to her but she told me she wasn't in love with me and she was bored with our life. She went on and on about how I disappointed her and she was done.

Within three weeks, she was gone. She took her things and half of what was in our bank account and moved in with her sister.

It has been difficult for me because despite our problems, it never occurred to me that she would leave. Every marriage has problems. People find a way to work out their problems but she didn't even want to talk about it. She just wanted to lay blame on me. It is all my fault that we don't have the white picket fence and 2.5 children. Forget that she also chose to work in a non-stable creative field. Everything was my fault.

I tried time and again to talk with her. I even told her that I would look into getting a "real job" if that's what it took to stay together. Her argument was that I would be miserable and in turn make her miserable. This makes me angry. She was being incredibly selfish and it seems to me that this was her excuse to leave me.

I didn't feel suicidal but I was very depressed. It was difficult for me to find my way out of being so down. My whole life changed in a short time. The rug was pulled from under me.

I cried. I talked to some female friends to try to understand a woman's perspective. I received different answers from my different friends. One argued how women need security and another said that Lynn just didn't want to be married to me anymore. That was painful to hear but I think that is the real reason.

I did talk to some of our mutual friends, specifically women. They were very careful to stay out of it. I asked for help, for reasons why she would do what she did but all I got was pity, so eventually I stopped.

I would drive by her house sometimes but I never looked for her online.

One friend gave me a number of a psychic, so I called. She saw Lynn moving away from me and getting remarried. She saw me getting remarried as well and that I will be by 2013. I wonder if she is right. I can't say that she made me feel better but I will have to wait and see.

Lynn walked out of our marriage a little over a year ago. About six months later I went on a date one of my friends had set up. I continue to see this woman and I am not sure where things will go. It is a help to have someone to be intimate with. Our relationship has become comfortable and I enjoy making love. Toward the end of my marriage, my wife and I were not having sex at all and I really missed it. I guess I figured we would find our way back to each other. I like being married and having someone to share my life with. But because of how my marriage ended, I am not sure if I should go in that direction. What if I invest my time and energy in another relationship only to be deserted again because I'm not Donald Trump?

At this point I am not sure what I would do if Lynn said she wanted to get back together. I still feel like I love her and we spent a very long time together but she hurt me. She left me in a cold way. She didn't want to work it out and I would be afraid that this subject would come up again, so there is no trust there for me.

From what I hear, she is dating someone. It hurts. It does help that I am seeing someone too. But I can't help but wonder what Lynn will do.

I am still working on feeling okay about it and am over the hardest part. I don't cry anymore and I'm not as angry. Time is the only thing that makes it easier. When it was fresh, it was awful.

If I could talk to her right now I would tell her that she gave up so fast. She is a selfish person who took advantage of a man who loved her. I thought she was my soul mate but now I really don't know about the whole idea of soul mates anymore.

I would like to feel that I would get married again. It scares me to think that women can just up and decide they are done with you and leave. I'm not sure.

34 Straight

My girlfriend had anorexia. We were together for five years. When we met, she was thin but not skinny. For a while I didn't know she suffered from this horrible disease. She didn't eat a lot. She would play it off that she wasn't hungry or had just eaten a big meal. The longer we were together, the more weight she lost and I finally started catching on. Her family lived in another state so no one was able to tell me about her problem. I found out later that her family didn't know.

It was hard to say anything to her. She would get very defensive and didn't want to talk about it. I would try to ease into it but she wouldn't even go there. She would get angry and start a fight about something else. I see now she was trying to take my attention away from her disease.

One time when we started to make love, her bones were sticking out and she complained that I was hurting her. I tried to be gentle but no matter what I did, she cried out in pain. We had to stop. I told her I knew she was going to get angry but I had to say something. I told her I thought she had a problem. She cried and told me I didn't understand and she was right. I had no idea how to deal with something like this. It was totally foreign to me.

She wound up in the hospital. She had passed out at work. Her parents flew in and when she was well enough to leave, they took her home with them. I wanted very much for her to stay with me but I could not argue with them. She weighed eighty-five pounds.

Her mom was kind enough to keep me posted on her health and it never improved. Within six months, she went down to seventy pounds and then her heart gave out on her. She died in her bed. Hundreds of miles from me. She was alone. It was the middle of the night. Every time I think of it, it brings tears to my eyes. I have no idea if she was awake and suffering, if she passed away in her sleep, no clue.

For a very long time, I was sad. I would cry. One of my close friends is a girl and I would talk to her about it. She would let me go on and on. Other men don't want that burden. They tell you they're sorry and that's pretty much all they can deal with.

It's been four years since she died. I am over the hard pain but I doubt I'll ever really be over losing her. I loved her and I felt helpless. I know it was nothing I did or could have done but when you lose someone you love to a disease that is self-inflicted, it is very hard to cope.

When she died, I would talk to her. I told her I was so sorry that she didn't see how to get better and how much I wished my love could have been the anchor for her to feel strong enough to stop starving herself. I also asked her to please help me deal with this so that I didn't always feel so sad.

> - **20% of people suffering from anorexia will prematurely die from complications related to their eating disorder**
> - **5-10% of anorexics die within ten years after contracting the disease**
> - **18-20% of anorexics will be dead after twenty years**
> - **30-40% ever fully recover – that's less than half!**
>
> teen-beauty-tips.com/national-statistics-for-anorexia

I went to counseling. My therapist encouraged me to keep a journal. Writing down what I felt really helped. It was a way for me to release the pain instead of finding unhealthy ways to deal with it. Talking about it to my therapist was also helpful. As our sessions continued, it was less about my grief and more about how I needed to move on in healthy ways. As a result, I no longer need to see him anymore. I've accepted that there will always be pain associated with my memory of her but it's a natural part of life to deal with grief. So I learned to manage my pain.

I didn't date anyone and didn't want to for two years. I now have a fiancé who I love. When I met her I was making an effort to get back into life. The timing was perfect. She was the first person I dated, so I guess I am lucky. We met at a Christmas party and I am so happy she came into my life. I have recently asked her to marry me and for some crazy reason she agreed. I was convinced I would never find love again. I am very grateful.

I believe in soul mates. I have met mine and I think that you can have many.

In closing, I just want to say if you or anyone you love is suffering from this horrible disease, I encourage you to seek help.

Sometimes the person with anorexia will not acknowledge they are sick and it is so important to not let them manipulate you into ignoring the problem. It doesn't go away on its own and it will kill you or someone you love.

THE OBSERVATION DECK

Psychologist

Dr. Billy Lee Kidd PhD
Senior Researcher, Romantic Relationship Institute, LLC
Portland, OR.
Featured on WebTalk and EZ Rock Radio
Author of *Low Stress Romance*

A little anthropological history:
Men and women respond the same way to a breakup. It involves a physiological process that is deep-rooted in our evolutionary system. Humans lived in small groups for the last five million years. You knew everyone and you struggled together to survive as a group. No one left and moved to another town. There were no towns and it was too dangerous to survive without your group. So you had to work it out and still be friends when you moved on to another partner. If a partner left and you never saw them again, it was because the person died. This is why it feels like you are mourning a death when a partner dumps you and breaks off contact. It triggers the mourning response.

    We all know that both men and women react with shock to an unexpected romantic breakup. They may appear to be on autopilot for a few days, their minds spinning with confusion. But in my fifteen years as a psychotherapist and couples counselor, I have noticed that this is where the similarities end. That is because men and women process their feelings about being spurned by a lover differently.

    After the shock settles in, women generally feel depressed. If that feeling lingers for quite some time, they want medication to treat it. Or perhaps, they turn to drinking to cover it over. Women may also internalize a sense of blame or a sense of being at fault for the breakup. Regardless, they stay in touch with their female friends and discuss what they are feeling—whether they are seeing a therapist or not.

    In contrast, men are more prone to feel a sense of distress and irreparable loss in reaction to the shock of an unforeseen breakup. Quite often, men deal with their distress by acting out. That might involve binge drinking, taking drugs or picking fights. Conversely, a man may withdraw from social contact or devote himself to his job and become a workaholic.

    Men are also prone to look for *the other man* to blame or to feel their ex-partner has a flaw in her character. They do this to deny responsibility for the breakup. When they are with their friends, men tend to minimize the pain they feel from the loss. But because of their acting out behaviors, they cannot hide their distress.

Some men, of course, experience depression after an unforeseen breakup. They are at a higher risk for committing suicide than are melancholic women. But overall, men tend to act out their troubles on life's stage rather than internalize their issues and feel depressed. This goes for gay and bisexual males, too. Compared to straight men, however, gay men tend to be more social about a breakup and want to talk to their friends about it.

Potentially, almost any man could act out and do crazy things to deal with his sense of distress over a breakup. It's common to see men move their social life to a bar and go on a drinking binge. Some end up in a hospital ER from alcohol and drug overdoses.

As a hospital therapist, I have dealt with men who have gone through this. One man, who came in tied down on a gurney with restraints, had uncharacteristically downed several hits of LSD in response to a breakup. Afterwards, he lay out on the sidewalk in front of his ex-girlfriend's apartment most of the night. At dawn, he followed a stray dog and spent a few days on the street with it, oblivious to his everyday responsibilities.

Another man, who had lived an otherwise normal life, hooked up with a heroin addict at a bar. He shot up for the first time with her, overdosed and nearly died. Yet another drank and drove his car at high speed. On a curve in the road, his car flew off and he was decapitated when it hit a tree.

Most men, of course, don't go to these extremes to deal with their sense of distress. It is common for men to simply rush into a rebound relationship, get married and pretend the whole thing was their ex's fault. This rebound blame game appears to cover over a man's sense of distress and his fear that the whole thing could happen again.

Sometimes, men acknowledge their sense of distress and seek help. Other times, their co-workers or their boss notes that something is wrong and suggests a visit to the company's employee assistance program. From there, they are referred to treatment.

When a man comes to my office, I try to normalize the situation. I do that by telling him: "You're not the first person to get dumped and you won't be the last. People always find a way to live through it. If you just show up here and talk to me, you'll get there. So this really isn't the end of the world. It just feels like it…OK?"

After a man acknowledges his sense of distress, I try to take the conversation beyond all that. To do it, I propose Move-On Question

Number One: "When this is over, and you're feeling OK, again, where would you like to be and what would you be doing?"

Most men answer the question immediately. One said he would like to end up somewhere like Hawaii, where there is sunshine and a beach. Another said he would like to have a new job. Whatever a man answers, we discuss it. Then, I ask Move-On Question Number Two: "What would you have to do to get there?"

Quite often a man's can-do attitude kicks in in response to that question. And then, he will tell me what it would take to fulfill his dream. After that, if he is willing, we spend some time every session working on achieving that dream.

If his goal is a meaningful, exciting new relationship, I still ask him the same question: "What would it take to get there?" One man answered, "I'd probably have to learn what a woman means when she tells me something because apparently I'm missing it." Later, he and I worked on communication skills.

Whatever happens during treatment, the important thing is to find ways to keep a man busy. The breakup feeling of distress hardly ever lasts more than six months. So if I simply provide enough emotional support to keep a man going, he'll work through his relationship breakup blues. If he's still distressed after six months, a man has other emotional problems holding him back. I will have discovered those by then and we will have already been working on those problems.

If a man has withdrawn from his friends and his normal recreational activities, I endeavor to get him to try something new. New activities stimulate a sense of meaning and purpose. If he cannot come up with a new activity, I suggest joining a fitness center, traveling or some activity involving other people, like tango or salsa dance groups.

I rarely suggest reading a book because most men will not bother to do it. If they do read it, they generally will not see the messages that are relevant to their situations. That's because when a man is distressed about a breakup, it's hard for him to believe that self-help books can ease his sense of loss. Rather, he wants immediate action—and immediate relief—not a promise for a better relationship down the road.

Some men will keep dating even while they are dealing with the sense of loss from the last relationship. What they do is go through their regular dating routines and pretend they're having a good time.

That's fine. It helps them to keep their minds off their problems. Yet they run the risk of repeating the last stress-filled relationship scenario all over again.

That is because they're too preoccupied with dating to learn the lessons the last relationship might have taught them. To avoid this possibility, I ask questions like, "Can you imagine trusting this person like a close friend?" or "Where are you picking things up emotionally in this relationship—like you are a teenager again?"

I generally do not ask, "How is this relationship different from the last one?" That is because a man will invariably say, "This is the right woman for me. The other one wasn't." That just kicks the can down the highway. Men say it to avoid taking responsibility for their relationship choices.

Interestingly, I find that young men are more prone to talk to their friends about their relationships than are older men. Young men know that the world is too complicated to do everything on their own. Besides, friends offer the best recourse for a heart that aches—activities that keep a man's mind focused on something besides his ex.

So, whatever the case, the cause or a man's age, he needs to keep busy after an unexpected breakup. That is what I would recommend to any man who is suffering from the breakup blues.

67 Straight

I married Lydia in 1969. I was twenty-five years old and she was twenty-three. We had been together for a year and a half and were full-fledged hippies. We met in college where the scene was sex, drugs and rock 'n' roll. We were no strangers to drug experimentation and all that went along with that time.

We had a large group of friends and partied all the time. One evening, at a party, the drugs were everywhere. Both Lydia and I took several different drugs including Acid, Quaaludes and Cocaine; add to that alcohol and Marijuana. I barely remember anything from that night. Prior to me getting completely wasted, I remember feeling excited about the idea that we were young and free. It didn't even occur to me that anyone could get hurt taking so many kinds of drugs. I was too busy having fun. We all were.

At some point during the evening, Lydia passed out and we joked about her being a lightweight. The rest of us who were awake continued to "have fun." The following morning, the room was filled with passed out, drugged partiers. When I woke up, or more accurately, "came to", I went to wake Lydia. She just laid there. I nudged her. I shook her. Nothing. She had passed away and we had no idea when. For all I know, when we initially thought she had passed out, she was already dead. I panicked and we called an ambulance.

That experience was devastating for me, to say the least. Not only did I lose my bride of only seven months, I blamed myself. I was there encouraging her to take a variety of drugs. She overdosed and it was my fault.

My life changed drastically after her death. It was difficult for me to function. I was so depressed. I didn't cry for two months but when I finally did, I sobbed and sobbed for what seemed like an eternity. Sometimes I would get physically ill, whether it meant actually throwing up or experiencing terrible stomach pains.

I continued to take drugs. When I wasn't high, I half wished that I would overdose. The guilt I felt was enormous and part of me wanted to die. I actually hoped I would. I missed her. She was my wife. I had never loved anyone so deeply.

I would dream of her and always wondered what the dreams meant. I wondered if it was just my mind or if she was actually visiting me. I questioned all the time and felt tortured every day. I thought about her constantly and it was extremely painful. I would often remember the good times we shared and for an instant, I could almost feel good but it seemed to make it worse. I was lost and didn't know how to be normal.

Fortunately, my parents were there for me. They took care of me when I was unable to cope. They insisted I attend therapy and I did. My therapist helped me in that he allowed me to express my pain. He encouraged it. I saw him for three years and I attribute my healing mostly to him.

The first year, I didn't date anyone nor did I want to. I didn't have it in me. Eventually, I allowed myself to try to get back out in the world. Much had changed within that year. I stopped taking drugs altogether. I volunteered my time to the less fortunate. I made an effort to really find a way to live and thrive as opposed to blaming myself for her death.

Though I found a way to work through my pain and grief, I have never completely gotten over what happened. I still think of her. Part of me still misses her, all these years later.

> *Since 1969, the first year Gallup asked about illegal drug use, Americans have grown increasingly more concerned about the effects of drugs on young people. For instance, in 1969, 48% of Americans told Gallup that drug use was a serious problem in their community. In 1986, a majority of Americans, 56%, said that the government spent "too little" money fighting drugs. By 1995, 31% said drug use was a "crisis" and an additional 63% said it was "a serious problem" for the nation as a whole.*
>
> Gallup.com/poll/6331/decades-drug-use-data-from-60s-70s

When I was twenty-nine, I met my current wife. I have a good life now. We have successful grown children and we are both retired. My wife knows about what happened with Lydia. I never told my children. That was another time.

Lydia still visits my dreams. Even though I am happy and have a great family, there is a sadness that lurks for what happened and what could have been. I was young but I was in love. Lydia was a tremendous woman who had a great joy for life. It makes me sad to this day to think of how her life was cut short. I remind myself that those were the times. We were doing what so many did, right or wrong.

Without a doubt, it was the hardest thing I have ever gone through.

No age given. Straight

I have gone through two breakups that were devastating to me. No one passed away but the pain I felt at the time was much worse than the pain I felt after my father passed away from cancer when I was fifteen. The reason for this was because I did not feel rejected by his death but after the breakup I did feel rejected.

We were together almost three years and were thirty days away from walking down the aisle.

It was difficult for me because I put everything I had into trying to make the relationship work and it still failed, or so I thought at the time. Ultimately, though, we were two good people who weren't good for each other.

I didn't try to get back together with her because we'd done that enough throughout our relationship. We'd be together, get engaged, break up, get back together, get engaged again—it was nuts! Looking back on it, I see my ex was saying things she didn't back up with her actions. I'm not placing blame; it's just the way it was.

I went through every emotion possible: I cried, I sobbed and moped around but at the end of the day, I was grateful because I knew if I had married her I would have been miserable.

It took a few months for me to begin seeing other people. After that experience my whole thought process about dating and relationships changed. I told myself I would never ask another woman to marry me if she couldn't give me what I needed to be able to spend the rest of my life with her. I used dating as a screening process to decide who I wanted to be in a relationship with.

I did engage in sex with the women I dated. It made me feel much better. After the breakup I took a step back to re-evaluate my role in what happened and to see what I had to do to make sure it never happened again. It most definitely helped. My ex and I barely had sex, which was devastating to my ego, so finding another woman who wanted to be with me, enjoyed being with me, was a big boost to my self esteem.

As I said, there were two loves that took me a long time to get over and both of them took about a year. Initially, I wanted to get them back but, as the saying goes, time heals all wounds. I realized with both women that they weren't the right ones for me.

I do admit to calling and hanging up, just to see if they were home but I soon realized that the more I knew, the more my wounds stayed open. I finally realized that the only way I could move on was to get them completely out of my life.

The most embarrassing thing I did was when I ran into the first woman who dumped me. It was at a big party. Her brother was a friend of mine and she was there. I was a complete asshole and said things to intentionally hurt her and show her that I'd moved on. It wasn't a classy move on my part and I apologized to her years later.

I never felt suicidal but I definitely hit rock bottom where I felt like if my life ended, it wouldn't be so bad.

My ex met a guy after she dumped me and I felt like was sucker punched when I found out. After all we'd gone through and all we had promised each other and talked about our future together, to find out she was interested in someone else was a huge blow to my ego. I felt like if I put my heart and soul into a relationship and it failed, there must be something wrong with me. Fortunately, I have a good family and friends who supported me and helped me to see it wasn't me; it was her.

I got over it by getting out there instead of wasting time and energy on what could have been. I started doing what made me happy at the moment. It was one of the best things I ever did.

There are people who help us experience a deeper and better part of who we are. I believe I have met my soul mate and feel that I am a better me because of the love and presence of my wife in my life. I do think we can have more than one soul mate in our lives. My mom got remarried after my dad passed and my step-dad is a wonderful human being. He'll never be my dad but we have a great relationship and my kids know him as Pop-Pop, not Nana's husband.

> ***A rejection is nothing more than a necessary step in the pursuit of success.***
>
> *Bo Bennett*
> *brainyquote.com*

31 Straight

I work with a woman. Her name is Kelly. In November of 2010 we were paired to work on a project together. I always thought she was pretty. We were acquainted with each other because of work but until we were paired up, we didn't really know each other. The project we were working on was laborious. It meant long hours working together and some weekends. As I got to know her more, I started liking her too much.

She has a boyfriend and she talks about him. He sounds like an asshole. He doesn't treat her with any respect. He has stood her up and doesn't attend any business functions of hers. He didn't come to the Christmas party with her and she was bummed about it. She tells me almost everything about their relationship. I hear the good with the bad and it is hard to act like I'm ambivalent.

I try to look for 'ins' when she goes on about him but hearing about how much she wishes he would do or be more for her is hard. I have fallen for her and think about her all the time. Every night before I go to bed and every morning when I wake up, she's on my mind.

The project we worked on is finished but we are still work friends. We have lunch together and email all during the day. She treats me like her friend. Sometimes she kind of flirts with me but I'm not sure if she is just being silly or if there is really something there. I can't really ask her.

Pain is a strong word. I am not sure that it's pain, although it is painful to me that I can't be with her. Once over the holidays, I had too much to drink and I went home and cried but it was more out of frustration. I had my phone in my hand ready to call her. I almost did. Thank GOD I was smart enough not to.

I mope sometimes on the weekends, especially on Saturday nights when I have no plans. I will go to bed early just to not be alone on Saturday night. I'll wonder what she's doing, if they are having sex, if she ever thinks about me. She has encouraged me to date and that made me feel like crap. She even mentioned that we could go on a double date. I would never be able to deal with that.

I have talked to a couple of women about this. Overall they tell me that because she has a boyfriend, I should let it go or find someone else to date. They will listen to me when I complain but they have no answers for me. Not answers I like anyway.

Since we started working together, I have only dated a few times. One here, one there. It never led to sex because they were just one time. I wasn't really interested in following up with these women. There is a woman who is my booty call and I have been with her. It helps but we are only about sex. We don't love each other and neither of us sees a future. We get together every once in a while when she is in town.

I wish all the time Kelly would break up with her boyfriend. We are already friends and I would at least have an opportunity to see if she likes me. We laugh a lot and have similar tastes and interests. I think if we had the chance, we could really fall in love.

We're friends on Facebook. I can see everything. I look at it often—not to spy—just because I'm already her friend. Sometimes she'll post new pictures of her and her boyfriend and that makes me feel uncomfortable.

> **We must embrace pain and burn it as fuel for our journey.**
>
> *Kenji Miyazawa*
> *quotegarden.com*

I would love to be able to tell her the guy she's with is a jerk and doesn't appreciate her. She deserves so much more. She deserves somebody who shows up for her, loves her and makes an effort. I don't get why women fall for the bad boy types and then complain about them. I am not a bad boy and I am not a doormat. I am just an average man who wants to get married and have a family. I want the woman I marry to be my best friend and I want to be good to her. But how can I say that to her? She would freak out. It isn't my place. All I can do is try, somehow, to move away from this. It isn't good for me.

45 Straight

When I was twenty-two I got my girlfriend Teri pregnant. We had been together a couple of years and we did love each other. We decided to get married. She was twenty. Even though we loved each other, we were too young and our decision to marry was based primarily on her being pregnant. We had no idea what we were getting into. Marriage is hard. When you're that young, you don't realize what it really means.

For us, it meant a lot of fighting. Our parents were helping us financially as I established myself in the working world. Money was always tight and led to many arguments. Eventually, I earned a good living, enough to support us but we still fought. We tried for the sake of our child but it eventually proved to be too much for us. I decided to leave. Even though she was very upset, we both knew staying together was not helping anyone.

Our divorce was hard. Our child was three years old and I felt an enormous amount of guilt. I knew I would always be a good father but I wasn't able to offer an ideal upbringing.

In the years after my marriage, I figured I would never remarry. It was too difficult and hadn't been a good experience for me. I dated a lot and had a few girlfriends.

Then I met Melissa. She was different. She was someone I really liked and we saw each other exclusively.

I believe I fell in love with her but never admitted that to her or myself. I was thirty-two and was set in the idea that I was not going to marry again. We were together for about a year or so and that topic came up. She asked me if I would get married again. I squirmed but told her I didn't see that for myself. She asked if I wanted more children and I said that I was open but had not really thought about it.

A short time later, she ended the relationship. She told me she wasn't going to stay with someone who she saw no real future with. I wasn't really sure what I wanted. I did want to be with her but I was so scared of going through another divorce. I tried to get her to change her mind but as long as I said I wasn't going to get married again, she didn't want to be with me. She explained that even though she didn't have to get married right away, she needed to know the possibility was on the table. So she walked away. I wanted her back but I was not ready to say that I would get married again.

As time went on, I began to date again but I really missed her. I thought about her all the time. I saw and had sex with other women.

The more I did, the more I thought about Melissa. I tried to contact her but she would blow me off, not answer her phone or not reply to my messages. I began feeling depressed. I felt so foolish letting her get away. The thought of her with another man made me feel anxious and jealous. I couldn't stand it. I didn't cry or sob but I wanted her back. I had to ask myself why I was so set on not getting married again.

The worst part about missing her was that I let someone I love go because I was afraid. I was afraid of getting hurt as well as hurting someone else. In the end, my fear of getting hurt, hurt me more than taking the risk. It isn't that I fell in to a deep depression; it was more a nagging feeling that I wouldn't be able to be with a woman who meant a lot to me. I decided that I could leave that open. I loved her. She was careful and didn't trust me for a while. She thought it was a matter of me wanting what I couldn't have. As it turns out, it was and is about genuine love.

> ***Marriage is the triumph of imagination over intelligence. Second marriage is the triumph of hope over experience.***
>
> *Oscar Wilde*
> *quotes4all.net*

We got married six years ago and have a three year old. We are happy. Melissa is my soul mate. She is my best friend and even though it was a rocky road, it gave us a strong foundation.

This was all before Facebook and I don't even have a Facebook account anyway. I never looked her up online nor did I call her and hang up. I did it the old fashioned way and just missed her a lot. I am glad she gave me another chance. If I would have allowed my fear to rule me, I would be miserable and most likely alone.

38 Gay

I was in a relationship with Jason for a little over five years. We lived together for three of the five years. We weren't married but lived like we were. We agreed that we would be monogamous. Jason is the love of my life. I met him was I was thirty-two and I loved my life with him. We spent a lot of time together. We took hikes, went for walks, went to dinner, the movies, friends' homes, all the things that couples do. I intended on spending the rest of my life with him. We talked about our future and planned for our old age.

Jason met another man at work. He told me he thought this guy was sexy and wanted to have a threesome. We had not engaged in anything like that before. The idea was thrilling to me but I had some reservations. I worried about STDs and the safety of it all. Eventually, I decided that we would try it. We did and it was good overall.

The problem I did not anticipate was the feelings associated with it. I figured it would be no more than a sexual release. For me, that's what it was. But Jason started to invite this other man to join us for casual things like dinner. It always turned sexual and I started becoming angry. I expressed my feelings to Jason and he argued that this was a good way for us to keep things fresh. But there was a real flirtation between the two of them and I was increasingly upset. Any time I brought it up, I was dismissed as being childish.

Eventually, this other man caused such problems in our relationship that I told Jason I didn't want him to be a part of our lives anymore. I wanted things the way they were. I asked Jason to attend counseling but he refused. I cried and we fought. Then I gave him an ultimatum. I told him that unless he was capable of going back to the way things were, I thought it would be best to split up. I honestly thought that would make a difference but to my surprise and disappointment, Jason agreed.

He moved out within two weeks and is now with that other man.

It is so hard for so many reasons. I am the one who broke things off, yet I am the one who really wanted the relationship to work. At first I would get angry with myself because I thought we might still be together if I kept my mouth shut. But I've realized that Jason was already very interested in this man. He wanted a way out and that kills me.

I called him many times. I saw him a couple of times too. Each time I tried to get him to reconsider. We had built a life, a good life, together and I couldn't understand how he could walk away. He later explained that for him, our relationship had become too constricted. He wanted to see other men and have sex with them. He knew I was too jealous to accept this. He actually told me he was doing me a favor because all he would wind up doing was hurt me over and over. He does not consider himself to be monogamous. He tried for me but it isn't how he wants to live his life.

> **Colleen Hoff at the Center for Research on Gender and Sexuality, San Francisco, recently published the Gay Couples Study. The study examined the relationships of committed gay male couples over a three-year period and found that 47% of gay couples have a "just in case" clause that specifically allows sexual activity with others. In 8% of the couples, one person favored an open relationship and the other expected monogamy. Of the respondents, only 45% described their relationships as monogamous.**
>
> crgs.sfsu.edu/research/gaycouples

I have cried a river of tears. It has been a couple of years since this happened and I am not as raw but it still really hurts. I love him and I want to be with him. I often speak to my friends about it. Everyone says the same thing, that I should get out there and meet other guys. They do listen to me but I am sure I am just a broken record.

In these two or so years, I have dated and had sex. The sex has differed. Some good, some okay but no one is Jason. I want so much to like someone else. I want to be excited but it hasn't happened. I am still working through getting over Jason. Every day I want him back.

I've called him and hung up, driven by where he lives, Googled him, spied on him on Facebook and Twitter and asked friends about him. I usually get upset when I hear he is doing well.

Once I felt suicidal. I was drunk. I wanted to take a bunch of pills. Luckily, I was too drunk to find them and passed out.

I imagine what they do and it makes me feel awful. I already know they have chemistry. I saw it, so it's easy for me to picture them together. When I remember all of us hanging out, I feel sick. My memories of the way they are together are too vivid and I hate thinking about it.

I have been in therapy for the last ten years. I talk about Jason almost every session and am advised to find other activities, to get out and meet people, to journal. I do all of that but I still feel very sad about it. Nothing will help. Unless I fall in love again, I think I will always miss him.

I believe in soul mates and mine is Jason. I hope that a person can have more than one because I would like to be married. I want to spend my life with a partner who wants that too. I hope I find it. I'm lonely.

THE OBSERVATION DECK

Psychic

Anne Temple
www.intuitiveannetemple.com
15 years experience

In many ways both genders have challenges dealing with heartbreak. It depends on the situation of the breakup.

Women usually want to feel that a man knows their pain; that he is aware he hurt her. Women also have a feeling that men will just go out and find another relationship right away. With death, women tend to go through a mourning phase with emotional release. In both cases women find it easier to talk with friends and family and are more apt to go through counseling.

Men, from my experience, have a hard time releasing a relationship emotionally. I feel that even when men break up with women they often have some remorse, feeling as though they could have fixed the relationship. Men's emotions are more internal than women's. Many times their friends will dismiss them. It's harder for men to go through or find counseling. Many times they will talk to a psychic more easily than to a professional counselor.

As for death, both men and women deal with it the same; yet I again find men not talking about their feelings. A divorce is like a death, especially when the relationship is long term. Divorce is harder for both genders in some ways because they have to deal with each other. Both genders tend to deal with breakups, heartache and death needing the same things: time, understanding and closure. I am seeing that both men and women have the same challenges yet express it in different ways.

Men call and generally ask more about financial guidance and less about heartbreak. They are more interested in love to be found, about if and when they are going to meet people, rather than breakups. The FUNNY thing about reading for men is when I have just read their girlfriends, wives or others, they always seem to want to know if she loves him. It's almost as if the readings are like a challenge—verging on asking who is better than the other. They test me more—try to trick me more. It rarely works but it is fascinating and funny how they stand back at first, reluctant, then really get into it. And THEN ask me about their financial situations. This is, of course, just a generalization. All my readings are different and of a personal connection with that person in regards to their situation.

From my experience, men are very different when it comes to

dealing with heartbreak. They don't talk with their friends and tend to internalize their emotions. They also seem to find it harder to let go of a relationship; wanting to find out how to reconnect, figure out what happened and fix it. Men seem to have a more difficult time being alone after a relationship. They experience a sort of separation anxiety and feel friendless versus women who have some anxiety yet can talk about it with friends and family. In many ways, our culture is biased, assuming that men will just get into another relationship or sexual connection faster than a woman. So in some ways, men will take longer to heal when they have heartbreak. Men may find a short-term relationship and try to reconnect with those feelings, especially when they feel they've lost a soul mate.

Men ask many of the same questions as women do about heartbreak—usually something about the future. They are sometimes flirtatious with me on the phone, not sexual but disarming.

They are just as obsessive about heartbreak as women. In this way, both genders are very much alike. I've dealt with a lot of situations where men obsess about their ex-girlfriends and ex-wives, getting overwhelmed with thoughts of the women taking them back. In some cases I've had men ask if they show up in the same places they know their ex will be, will the ex take them back. I discourage this behavior! Men *and* women may do this just the same. In many instances men listen less to my advice and predictions of where this will lead them and they go and do it anyway. I guess the only thing I can say about that is we all are born with free will. Men also will try calling or e-mailing their ex, asking how they're doing! Just like women, men want to reconnect and it can take years to get over heartbreak, especially when a man thinks that this woman is his soul mate.

When the relationship goes sour and even when men break off the relationship, a lot of my patrons will try to make the women feel some reconnection by asking them out for lunch. Even when men try to move into a new relationship years later, they'll try to call an ex to get back into a relationship. In our culture we hear about restraining orders. This isn't just about abusive behavior. There's a fine line and men as well as women cross these boundaries.

I don't see many men cry in readings. On the phone men will talk openly and rarely cry, whereas in a live reading they are emotional and I see more tears but not a full cry. Men are more open to disclose that they cry when alone but not in front of me, just teary-eyed emotion.

Men often do not want to react or argue. In many ways men's voices will get very cold. They'll just disconnect from me right away, trying to not argue. They seem very disappointed. Yet they will call over and over, getting readings as many times as women. Men will want to know if she is going to come back. As a professional reader I try to discourage this repetitive calling with both men and women. I find it doesn't help them get over or through the issues they are dealing with.

Men often ask: Has she cheated on me? Why did she leave me? Can I fix the relationship? Will she come back? Will she leave me? Is she with another man? When will I meet another woman?

Depending on the type of loss, both genders have a hard time with love lost. I talk with both women and men who stay in a bad relationship and go through a grieving period in a relationship. I find many people thinking that more women call me than men, yet this isn't true.

Women think men don't feel the same and will just go out and get another woman right away. I find this to be a cultural bias; the truth is that women will find a new relationship faster than most men. I talk with both genders from all over the world and find the same to be true in most countries and cultures.

Then we have love lost within alternative relationships. Men tend to move on faster than women. In these relationships women will try to work things out with their partners more but it can be highly emotionally charged.

Overall, I hope this will enlighten readers. We all, men and women, during times of change feel loss, emotionally depressed and hurt. I find we all have the same fears. We all want to find our soul mates.

51 Straight

I've gone through two breakups that were devastating to me. The first was in high school. She was my first crush. It was absolutely fantastic. When I saw her I couldn't speak, walk or look into her eyes. It was both mortifying and stimulating. But it was high school.

The second time happened recently. I was with her for five months. We weren't married and had no children, however we were both married to other people.

It was a four-month flirt, a one-night affair and two weeks of vibrant communication. We broke up because we knew if we kept going it would explode in our faces. People would get hurt and we didn't want to be responsible for that.

We love each other without limit. We met, the pheromones flashed; we flirted, dallied and fell in love. What a fantastic experience. We tried very hard to hang on to the chaotic excitement generated by our paring but it was impossible. Our situation was too complicated.

I didn't make any promises to try to lure her back, although I totally lost my mind and proclaimed many affirmations and professions of my love for her. We were cheaters but we honestly loved each other. We professed our undying devotion for each other and relayed the pain we felt because of our separation. There was no need to make artificial pledges.

I expressed my pain by sending her beautiful, handwritten poetry. I cried a lot and openly sobbed. I spilled my guts to her so prodigiously that I embarrassed myself. I told her I'd wait for her forever and that I planned to marry her some day. I became so obsessed I drove her away.

To get away from the pain, I buried myself in my work, as much as I could anyway. I needed to talk to someone, so I confided in my older brother, whom I knew I could trust.

There was no one else after her. As I said, I'm married and I cherish my wife. I know—I'm a cad. Forgive me. I desperately tried to repair my marriage and instill a spark of romance into it. But my love for my wife didn't help. I haven't taken a breath without wondering if the other woman and I will get another chance at love.

I haven't snooped around in her life or tried to call her but I have Googled her name about a dozen times.

We were both married and we entertained our selfish desires. I didn't even know her husband but every time I sensed him even having coffee with her I felt overwhelmingly jealous. I wanted her for myself and the fact that it was out of my control nearly broke me. I felt like someone had cleaved my heart in two. I laid my neck bare for her because I felt she was ready for it. It was a foolish mistake. I've felt desperate, yes, but never suicidal.

I'm still experiencing acute pain. When I finally get to the point where I feel okay about it, it will be due to a lifetime of protection measures—internal barriers I can erect when threatened spiritually. I feel the walls rising already and they are heavily fortified.

In my heart, I know that woman is my soul mate and I know she feels the same about me. I'm about to take my wife on an anniversary trip. How's that for irony?

The outcome of this fling has been intensely painful but our brief affair released feelings I thought I'd never enjoy again. Even with the negative consequences, to experience the uncontrollable wave of hyper-infatuation and then fall desperately in love, well, I'm just so glad it happened. We both bathed ourselves in waves of romantic love that had long since left our respective marriages. We parted and I don't see any further communication or visitation but I want her to know that she touched me deeply. I will never forget her and I will love her until the day I die.

> **People who are so dreadfully "devoted" to their wives are so apt, from mere habit, to get devoted to other people's wives as well.**
>
> *Jane Welsh Carlyle*
> signs-of-a-cheater.com

68 Straight

This is very difficult for me to write. After more than six years I still mourn and the tears come flooding back as I write but I feel the story must be told. We met in a bar. That's right, in a bar. I was twenty-four and working in my mother's beer bar as a bartender. It was a small but cozy place. It had twelve stools at the bar, four tables surrounding the coin-operated pool table and a small dance floor in the back with a tight little raised stage for a band. On Saturday nights a western band, and I use that term loosely, played loudly. The loudness covered the bad music and even worse singing. One time a customer came in and said he was from Los Angeles, eighty miles to the north. He said he came down especially to hear the band. After asking why, he replied; "I've heard it's the worst band in Southern California and I just had to see for myself." He wasn't disappointed. But it was home.

During the day I played pool for beers. At that time beer was only a quarter for draught and since I didn't drink on the job, when I won, I would win a quarter. I was pretty good and usually won more money than I was paid for bartending. Well, one day I'm standing behind the bar when two girls I've never seen before walked in. They both ordered draught beer. I checked the ID of one girl, Angela, and figured that the other girl was over twenty-one so I didn't check her ID. I found out later she was only twenty. Neither of them was anything outstanding, so after I served the beers I turned around and began washing glasses.

As I washed I sang quietly to myself along with a Jim Reeves record that was playing on the jukebox. Angela spoke up saying, "Sing a little louder, I like your voice." This shocked me a bit because no one had ever asked me to sing louder. Some had asked me not to sing at all but never louder. I stopped singing and turned around to take a better look at this crazy girl who wanted to hear me sing. She wasn't beautiful, though she was pleasing to the eye. She was 5'1" tall according to her ID. She had brownish blonde hair, green eyes and a beautiful smile. The more I looked at her, the prettier she looked. I finally decided that she was very pretty. I said, "Why in the world do you want me to sing?" Angela replied; "I think you have a beautiful baritone voice and I like music. Please sing some more." After we had introduced ourselves she played a dozen songs on the jukebox as I sang along.

I was glad the two girls were the only customers. I don't think I could have handled anybody else listening in. We talked for a while and then her girlfriend said she had to go. Since Angela was riding with her, they both left.

Two days passed without Angela coming in. I had pretty much forgotten about her when she walked through the door alone. She was dressed very nicely and had just had her hair done. Now she was stunning. I couldn't believe that I had once found her looks rather common. We talked for hours until closing time. Before she left I asked for a date. She accepted and the race was on.

We had been dating for about eight months when I proposed. We set a date for the following February, about six months away. I needed the time to come up with the money to buy the rings. Bartenders don't get paid much and I didn't want a cheap gold band, nor did I want to make payments on the rings. That would just be too tacky. We were married on February 11, 1966. We started a home together in a small apartment and were very happy. About eight months into the marriage Angela became pregnant. Two months later she miscarried. We were both devastated but knew we could try again. She never became pregnant again.

We finally took a long, eight week vacation in 1970 and drove eighty-six hundred miles around the country seeing relatives on both sides of the family. I had just graduated from apprentice school and was a journeyman plumber and we could afford it. It was our belated honeymoon. It seemed like everywhere we stopped something would break. At one stop in South Carolina we washed our clothes and her aunt's washer broke down. In Iowa at another aunt's house the bed we were sleeping in broke and the mattress came crashing to the floor. We got out of bed and replaced the fallen slats but the moment we climbed into bed the slats fell out again and we crashed to the floor a second time. We decided to leave the mattress on the floor and had a good nights sleep. In the morning, downstairs at breakfast, no one said a thing about the loud crashes during the night. We finally told our aunt that the bed was broken and explained the whole thing. Everyone seemed to have a sense of relief on their faces. Our aunt said that the crashes had awakened everyone but they didn't want to say anything. After all, "Who knew what you were doing up there."

Five years later, Angela had gained about twenty pounds and the doctor told her she had Type II diabetes. She had to take insulin shots and that gave her a tendency to gain more weight. Later she started developing other problems related to diabetes.

By 1978 I started my own plumbing business and was doing

quite well. I had never seen Angela so happy. We were not poor anymore. Angela had the car of her dreams, a 1979 Chrysler Cordoba. She had many friends from our Elk's Lodge and was enjoying life to its fullest. In 1981 I lost the business due to my partner going off his rocker and I went back to work for someone else.

In 1983 Angela began having great pains in her abdomen. She was diagnosed as having ovarian cancer. The doctor explained that the miscarriage had injured her uterus and this was the reason she had been unable to get pregnant. The cancer was a result of problems due to the diabetes.

Angela required surgery. After the hysterectomy she received radiation therapy and was finally pronounced clear of the cancer. Although we both loved children, we knew we could never have them. Angela was a person who loved life and everything and everybody. She never met anyone she didn't like. She was bound and determined not to let her illness get her down.

As time went on her diabetes caused more problems. She developed deep sores on the bottoms of her feet and found it difficult to walk. Yet she still kept her spirits up. In Late August of 2004 she collapsed at work and her co-workers called me. I instructed them to call the paramedics and said I would get there as soon as possible. The paramedics said her blood sugar had dropped to dangerous levels but that she was stable now.

She started watching her blood sugar more closely and seemed to improve. A few weeks later she developed strong stomach pains and I took her to the emergency room. At the hospital we were told that Angela had kidney problems. They kept her in the hospital for a week and then sent her to a nursing facility to recuperate. In the nursing facility she got worse. They even talked of amputating her left foot. In early December I received a call from the nursing home. She was having chest pains and had been sent back to the hospital. At the hospital I was told that her heart was not well. It was only pumping about half what it should be.

While in the hospital, she seemed to get better and my niece visited at Christmas and set up a small tree with decorations. We celebrated and sang songs and Angela talked of visiting her sister in Washington State in the summer. She was getting better.

One week later she suffered a heart attack and was brought back by electric shock and CPR. She was then sent to ICU for careful observation. She had another heart attack in ICU. She never recovered.

She died on January 10th 2005. She was sixty-one years old. I thank God for the forty years we had together. They were wonderful years and she never gave up on life. She was always happy and tended to the woes of others as though she was completely healthy. She loved people, she loved animals and she loved nature. And most of all, I know she loved me.

I think of Angela often. I cried often after her death and still do occasionally. At first the only images that came to mind were of her suffering and death. Then, as the months went by, I began to remember the good times. We had a lot of good times, despite her illness. She enjoyed life so much. I often miss her when I am cooking. We were both accomplished cooks. I used to joke with her and tell her that was the only reason I married her, because she was a better cook than I. Now when I cook one of her favorite recipes and can't fully remember what she used, I almost call out her name to get the recipe. I often find myself waiting for her to come through the door singing out, "I'm home." But alas, it never happens.

I have learned to cope, but I will never forget her. She is always with me.

I leave you with these words. Every day let your loved ones know that you love them. Don't assume they know. Tell them so. You never know when God will decide to take them. Goodbye and God bless you, Angela. I'll see you later.

> *Goodbyes are not forever.*
> *Goodbyes are not the end.*
> *They simply mean I'll miss you*
> *Until we meet again!*
>
> Author Unknown
> quotegarden.com

30 Straight

About a year ago, my girlfriend broke up with me. We were together for just over two years. I don't understand why she left. She said she wanted to have her freedom, that she felt suffocated. I had no idea if this is what she was thinking. She never talked about it with me. She made her decision and that was it.

It was hard because I thought everything was fine. I thought she was happy. I was happy. I like being in a relationship and I liked being in one with her. It makes no sense to me that someone just changes her mind. I know she must have been unhappy for a while but she never talked to me about any of it.

I tried for a while to get her back. I would ask her to meet with me and she did. Her eyes were lacking in any enthusiasm. She treated me like I was a chore. It hurt. I asked her what I could do to make things better. She told me there was nothing either one of us could do. She wasn't interested in keeping the relationship alive because she was not happy. I asked her how long she had been feeling that way and she told me it didn't matter. I was angry when she said that. Why was it all about what she thought? I was fifty percent of the deal and I was cut off and had no option.

> **Relationships are like glass. Sometimes it's better to leave them broken than try to hurt yourself putting it back together.**
>
> *Anonymous*
> quotations.about.com/od/sadquotes/a/breakup

I cried a little at first. I was mostly shocked. I tried to think of ways to make it right. I would think about what had been going on in the last year of our relationship and see if I could figure out what happened to make her leave me. Other than typical couple problems like bickering or mood swings, I couldn't figure out what had changed so drastically.

Sometimes I still try to remember and replay our last year. I remember a lot of the good and it only confuses me more. Right before she left, we had attended a wedding. She "played" the role of being very happy. She was holding my hand, we danced, and we kissed.

I had messages from her on my cell phone and I used to play them over and over right after she left. I finally erased all of them and took the pictures we had to my parents' house and put them in a box in the garage. I would look at them and feel worse. I had to remove all the things that reminded me of her from my home. It made me too hopeful and sad at the same time.

I wonder if she met someone else. That is the only conclusion I have to the "why" of it. But I don't know for sure.

I started dating other people several months after she broke things off. I was having a hard time. Feeling sorry for myself and low. As I mentioned, I like being in a relationship. I am bored and lonely when I am not in one. It helped in a small way. It's nice to get attention and have dates to go on. It's great to have sex. Not that I had so much sex but I did find getting out helped me to feel better about things.

I admit, I did call and hang up a few times early on but eventually I saw it was immature, so I stopped. I also figured she knew it was me. I would do it so she would call me and ask if I called her. She never did.

I don't think I was desperate. I was lonely, sad and very confused. I wouldn't kill myself over this or anything. It is my belief that suicide is wrong.

I withdrew for a while and slept a lot. That isn't like me. I usually am fine with five or six hours of sleep a night. For the first few months, I slept nine or more hours at night and took naps on the weekends. I did it to escape. I don't really enjoy drinking and do not take drugs.

It took six or seven months for me to not be sad about it. At that point, I was able to not think about her or the situation all the time. Even though it did still hurt, it wasn't consuming me. Enough time has gone by now and I don't care as much. I have been seeing a woman for the past two months and I am hopeful about her. It definitely makes it easier for me.

Now that I am with a woman I really like, I feel much better. It helps to have someone new and fresh. It takes away the loneliness. What my ex did hurt me but I was able to move past it.

I would very much like to get married. I feel most content when I have someone to share my life with. It is too soon to tell if the woman I am seeing will ever be my wife but it is a goal I seek.

48 Straight

My wife and I had a business and a home that we were both invested in financially. We were married for thirteen years. Around year ten our marriage started to change. We argued. We weren't getting along. We experienced financial stress due to the economy. It became apparent that neither one of us wanted to be married to each other anymore. We went to a therapist. After ten or so months, all three of us agreed that the marriage had no place to go.

The problem was money. My wife and I could not afford to move out. Our money was tied up in the business and in our home that had lost value and we had to figure out what to do. We decided to continue living together and tried to stay out of each other's way. For the most part it was doable but it was pretty frustrating. We both were eager to get out and experience the freedom we longed for. Once the decision was made that the marriage was over, there was a relief but because we still had to live together, it was tough for both of us.

> *In a survey conducted by the National Marriage Project at the University of Virginia, it was found that nearly 40% of married Americans between the ages of 18 and 45 who had been considering divorce put aside those plans due to the recession.*
>
> *www.virginia.edu/marriageproject*

During the time my wife and I were trying to deal with the business and sell the house (this was 2007-2010 NOT THE BEST TIME TO SELL!!!!), I met Diane through a mutual friend at a dinner party. We connected. I was honest about my living situation but I made it clear that I was interested in her and I wished to see her.

She agreed to be my friend. She said that even though she believed me, she wasn't getting involved with a married man. I was quite aggressive in getting to know her. She was so vivacious, smart and funny, unlike many women I knew. (Not that I don't know smart women, it's just the combination she has.) We would essentially date without anything physical. An old-fashioned courtship if you will.

After about six or seven months we both gave in and had sex. It was great. We indulged a few times but then she pulled away. I still didn't know how long it would be until I was free and she couldn't take it. My wife and I had filed for divorce at that point and were in the process but Diane was uncomfortable and I couldn't blame her. She basically broke up with me. Because we had crossed the line with sex, she didn't know how to continue seeing me like we were just friends. I pleaded with her to be patient and reminded her that I was getting a divorce. But she insisted. Until I was divorced and moved out, it was better for her to not see me anymore and she asked that I not contact her. From that point on, our contact was limited to mostly email and very infrequent phone calls. As much as I tried to not call her, I had to from time to time.

I was pissed now. I resented my wife, although this was not her fault. I was angry with the government (still am) for making my life so goddamned difficult financially. I missed Diane.

It took about seven or eight months before I was divorced, moved out and ready to go. I did what she asked. There were plenty of times when I wanted to call and tell her I was moving out in three weeks—but she said she wanted me to be free. So I waited.

When I contacted Diane, she seemed surprised and told me she was seeing another man. She explained that she had not been totally convinced I was ever going to leave my wife, that there were too many liars out there so she felt that when an available man presented himself, she wasn't going to wait for the one she wasn't sure about.

Needless to say I was upset. My heart sank, my ego was blown and I was angry. She told me she had been dating this guy for about five months and things were going well. She said she didn't want to say anything to me because she didn't want me to think she was baiting me or lying to make me move faster to leave my wife.

It wasn't an official breakup or even an official relationship. I don't know how to describe what we had but I developed feelings for her. I love her. When she told me she was with another guy, I felt like I was body slammed. I am so jealous to think that another guy gets to be with her and I can't.

I tried very hard to convince her that her relationship with this other man was still new and she could give me a chance. But she said no. They were a couple and it wouldn't be fair to him. That made me pissed! He got her. It wasn't fair to me. She ASKED me to wait until I was free. I DID WHAT SHE ASKED!

I didn't cry or sob. I did tell my good/best friend (male) what happened but I don't talk about it all the time. I think about her all the time, though. I mean all the time. This went down in September 2010. It is now February 2011 and it feels like it just happened. I think about her constantly and it makes me feel weak. I keep hoping she will call me and tell me she's free but she hasn't.

I have dated. It helps during the date. It's good to talk to someone else and maybe have a nice time. But sometimes I find myself comparing my date to Diane and they never seem to be as great. I would like to find a woman who I can be in a relationship with but I haven't yet.

I have had some sex. I can separate and enjoy sex but I also want to be sexual with someone I love. I think that is how Diane affected me most. I was attracted her but I also felt affection for her. I wanted more than sex.

I am still not over Diane. I hope she surprises me soon and lets me know she's free.

I want her back all the time.

I have looked her up on Facebook. But her profile is closed. We used to be Facebook friends but she took me off.

I feel sick to my stomach every time I think about it. I can't blame her for what she did but it really fucks with my head to think of her with another man.

I am no longer married. I assume I will marry again but I will make sure that I feel it really is the best choice. I know now what it is to be in a marriage that doesn't work and I really don't want to go through that again.

Diane, please choose me!

34 Straight

The most devastating breakup I went through was with an older, married woman.

We met through work. I am in sales and she was my client. There had been flirtation the whole time we conducted business. When the deal was made and I no longer had a reason to visit her anymore, I offered to take her to dinner to celebrate the close of our business. As soon as we sat down to eat, we both knew what the outcome of the evening would be. She was forty-six and had been married for many years. I guess she was bored.

After dinner, we ended up at my place. We had wild sex for hours. She was like no woman I had ever been with. Not only was she smart; in bed she was UNBELIEVABLE! Our chemistry was potent and it ignited a full-blown affair.

As our relationship continued, she told me that while she felt friendship for her husband, she was no longer attracted to him. She also told me she had not cheated on him before and this is why the sex was so incredible.

> *I think I could fall madly in bed with you.*
>
> Author Unknown
> quotegarden.com

We were together for about a year and saw each other a few times a week. Her husband traveled a lot for work, so she had the time. As we progressed in our relationship, I started to fall in love with her. For the majority of the time, I kept this to myself. When I finally admitted this to her, she told me she liked me a lot and cared for me but that for her, this was something on the side that she enjoyed but could never be anything more. She looked at me like I was a sad puppy. Not only was I upset that she didn't feel love for me but the fact she felt pity for me was humiliating. I tried to stop seeing her but it was hard. I would give in and then I would start wanting more again, so she finally ended it.

I tried many times to get back together with her. There were a lot of times she saw me and we wound up in bed together. I would always hope that this time she would tell me she loved me but she never did.

I cried when I was alone. My friends knew I was seeing someone but I never told them she was married. I hid my pain and that made it worse. I couldn't (and still can't) understand how someone could be so cavalier—especially a woman. It's always been my understanding that women are the ones who get emotional. That is another humiliating aspect to me. I took on the role of the woman.

I dated from time to time during the relationship, just because I wanted to have options. When we broke it off, it was hard for me to date. It took many months; I'm not sure how long. I loved her and seeing other people only made me want her more.

I think it was about six months before I finally dated others and had sex. It did help. When I met my current girlfriend, I was able to get over the affair in a more complete way.

I used to want her back daily. I am in a good relationship now so I am not interested in getting back with her. I was angry for a long time but now I see it as something that helped me understand myself.

I admit to calling her and hanging up, as well as Googling her name online. I don't think she has a Facebook page.

The most embarrassing thing was I showed her my feelings. I let her see that I was vulnerable. For her, our relationship was much less. I thought she would eventually leave her husband and she and I would be together. I feel so stupid that I ever thought that!

I didn't feel suicidal. There were times I felt desperate but not in a harmful way. I was just really sad.

I don't know if there's such a thing as soul mates. If there is, I don't think I've met mine. I would like to be married. The woman I'm with - I love her and she loves me. I think we are headed towards marriage.

The Observation Deck

Bartender

Belinda

I have been tending bar for six years. I work in a watering hole, meaning it's not a dive. It's not a hip club. It's old school. It smells like old beer and cigarettes. We serve crap fried food, have a jukebox and the customers range in age from twenty-one to eighty.

Over the years I've seen a lot of men who have gone through some kind of breakup. Some widowers too. I don't really see gay men here so I can't accurately give my opinion there.

From what I see with men who are dumped, they are a mess. They come here and their attitude is quiet. They'll get a few drinks in them and they can go in different directions. It's usually some combination of these situations: They get drunk and cry to me. They ask me: Why didn't she love me? They ask if I ever dumped my man and they look for the answer they want to hear. Did you call him? Did you miss him? Did you sleep with other men? They can also get highly flirtatious with every woman, including me. To the point that it's nauseating. They are looking to stroke their egos and, if they are lucky, something else. They need to know someone finds them attractive. Often, because they are drunk and acting like a jerk, they don't go home with a woman. Sometimes, they find women who are just as drunk or insecure and they make the hook-up. They will be all over each other all night. It's funny because if they both wind up back at the bar later, they will not even acknowledge each other. I guess that is more sad than funny.

Sometimes they will sit quietly, keep to themselves and drink. They will say something negative about relationships from time to time. But mostly they observe.

You have the guys who have JUST been dumped. They are looking to fight. They will deliberately go and flirt with a woman who is with another man. They're looking for someone to fight with so they can get out their anger. Not all men react this way but there is a group of men who look to fight. We have had to call the cops tons of times on these kinds of guys. One time a couple was in the bar and the guy needed to use the bathroom. Dumped, drunk "Sam" came over and started hitting on her. He was being lewd and making a big play for her. Her man came back and "Sam" continued to flirt, asking why she would stay with the guy she was with (in front of the guy). This gave her poor boyfriend no choice but to defend his fair maiden. Punches flew, "Sam" lost a tooth that night and they were both arrested. It doesn't happen every night but I would guess there are fights every couple of months and that is why we hired a doorman who is 6'5".

The worst (in my opinion) are the older widowers. They are regulars. Sometimes they cry. Sometimes they're in a good mood but they are so lonely and it's sad. They have no one and the bar is the only place they have where they feel like they know someone. Not looking for love, more like drinking until they die. I feel bad for these guys. I always think of them on major holidays when the bar isn't open. I wonder what they do because they are ALWAYS here the day after a holiday.

When a man is dumped, sometimes he will come in the bar, sit down, get a drink and he opens up to me about what happened. He is the guy looking to a female he doesn't really know for answers. I am his shrink. He wants to know what he did wrong. These men will often confess something to me. They had been unfaithful or they weren't attracted to her anymore—whatever. They are not the flirters or the fighters. They are sad and lonely and looking to fill up time and maybe figure something out.

I see men dealing with a broken heart all the time. The difference I have seen with women is that the girls come in ready to party and flirt. Their ex is an "ASSHOLE" and they have their girlfriends around them to support that. They say, "HE'S AN ASSHOLE!!! FUCK HIM!!!" They drink to that. They dance to that. They flirt with other guys. They try, at least for that one evening, to be strong. They laugh loud and hard and drink too much. They all bond with each other to show the world they won't be defined as the sad chick staying home on Saturday night eating and hoping he'll call. They do that Sunday through Friday.

To me, men seem weaker. They are so confused and feel they can only talk to strangers. They fight, they have meaningless sex, they look for answers from me and other bartenders. They are sad and pathetic.

Obviously men and women both have a hard time losing love. Because I am a woman who has been dumped and has girlfriends who have also been dumped, I know what women do. How they feel. We have the benefit of freedom to express ourselves. Even though the women at my bar are laughing too loud, I think it's that they grieve all week. They talk about it with their girlfriends, they have an outlet and the bar is a place to go and blow off steam. It's a place to forget their troubles, kick off their shoes and scream, dance and act like teenagers.

Manufactured fun.

The bar is one of the only places some of these men have to help raise their self- esteem. NOT a good idea. But they probably are not on the phone for three hours with a buddy dissecting everything about the relationship. They are sucking it up. The bar is their only refuge. And most of the time, they come across as sad puppies with no idea of how to go about getting over the woman who broke their heart!

65 Straight

I was married to Gloria for forty-two years. We have three grown children. We married when we were both in our twenties. Marriage isn't easy. It's hard. There were times in my marriage that I wasn't sure if we would make it. We attended couples therapy for a few years and that helped. I thought we had a good thing despite some of the harder times.

Last year Gloria told me she wanted a divorce. I didn't understand where this came from. We had been doing fine (in my estimation) for years. Sex had dwindled but I figured that is to be expected. We would have it but it was infrequent. I asked her why and she told me that she had been unhappy for a long time. I asked why she hadn't addressed this before. She said she saw no point. She had fallen out of love with me and stayed because she was too scared to move on alone.

I tried to get her to agree to counseling. I told her that I would do whatever it took. I was angry and scared. Scared that now I would be alone in my old age. She didn't want to try. She had made up her mind and soon after, she rented an apartment and left.

I found out she had connected with her high school boyfriend on Facebook and they are now seeing each other. I am devastated. When she left, it was hard enough but finding out she is with another man has put me in such a horrible state of mind.

In the time since we split, I have had an extremely difficult time. At my age, the thought of trying to find love and trust is very scary. I was content in our marriage and have no desire to live out the rest of my life alone.

I am also retired and because of the divorce, I have lost quite a bit of money and find it necessary to get back into the work world. I have been putting that off but it is something I must address soon.

I spend most of my time alone, which isn't helping me. I have family and friends to turn to and spend time with but mostly I keep to myself. I try to keep busy with hobbies but I only feel I am biding my time.

I have cried but not a lot. I think a lot about how I should change my circumstances. I don't want to live out the rest of my life being some lonely old man.

I haven't dated anyone. My friends have tried to set me up but I'm not comfortable with that idea.

I want Gloria back and that's no secret. I don't believe she will come back to me. She told me she isn't in love with me anymore and that was a crushing blow. When you have been with someone for so long, the love changes. It is no longer new; it becomes comfortable and something you feel you can count on. When it is pulled out from under you, especially in your sixties, it feels like defeat. Finding out that she is with someone else is terribly painful. Not only does she have a life that she wants, she is in love or thinks she is. She is feeling great and I am alone and fearing my life as an old man alone.

I can't imagine getting married again. I know people at my age find each other but I don't have the energy. I liked my life the way it was.

> *A divorce is like an amputation: you survive it, but there's less of you.*
>
> *Margaret Atwood*
> *thinkexist.com*

No age given. Straight

I have been through two breakups, both involving marriages and both of which affected my career. My first marriage lasted eleven years and produced two children. My second marriage lasted for eighteen years, although our relationship spanned twenty-six years. During that marriage I acted as a stepparent to three children.

The first breakup was due to my affair with "the other woman" whom I subsequently married and also because my wife was having an affair as well. I had to leave my children behind and move to a new town quite a distance away from them. I worked as a disc jockey and attempting to entertain the listeners while feeling so sad was extremely difficult.

It didn't take me long to get over my first marriage but that's because I was involved with the woman who would become wife number two. I dealt with the pain of having to leave my children behind by burying myself in my on-air activities as well as having the comfort of my new lover.

I did make an attempt to get back together with my first wife and we actually did reunite and managed to sustain the marriage for a few years with no contact from my former lover. However, she resurfaced some years later, which reignited the romance and caused the eventual end of my first marriage.

I learned that my first wife found other male interests but they, for the most part, including three marriages, didn't last very long. In fact, one of her married partners called and asked me for help in understanding her because she was somewhat off the wall. I kind of felt sorry for the poor guy, who eventually divorced her and remarried.

To this day I still occasionally have regrets and secretly wish I could get my first wife back. We married so young and hadn't allowed our minds to develop and mature and also because of the children.

Getting over my second marriage was more difficult. I left my first wife for the woman whom I thought was my soul mate but she turned out to be the determining factor in ending my broadcasting career. Our breakup was due to conflicting views on what my relationship should or should not be with my own children. However, I believe there were many underlying reasons for that breakup.

Here's the spicy part. My second wife, whom I met while still married to my first wife, was also married and, at the same time as she was seeing me, was also seeing another person. After we'd been seeing each other for more than a year, she became pregnant with her other lover's child, which her husband assumed was his. Once we were married, I, with the full knowledge that one of her three children was her ex-lover's, raised that child as my own. To this day, that child isn't aware of that fact, nor is anyone else.

The pain resulting from the end of my second marriage was much more intense and required group counseling, where I learned that all of the blame I had inflicted upon myself was not my fault. Group sessions allow one to compare instances similar to yours and see how others reacted as well as allowing you to vent your own feelings and finally resolve those issues within yourself. Those sessions helped me to get over the marriage, get on with my life and finally realize that I could exist without a relationship. I cried a lot and walked along the beach at sunset for months, thinking and just losing myself in the salt sea air.

I never felt suicidal. Not with my first wife and not with the second. I'm always looking at the fact that tomorrow might bring an experience worth living for.

I didn't begin to see other people at all; at least I didn't attempt to strike up any sort of a relationship. I think I had just about had it with trusting and thinking that any woman was worth the risk. I never made any outward advances towards any woman but in reality the reverse occurred. They made advances towards me. I assume this was due to the fact that I am an outgoing individual who openly expresses my feelings and this seems to attract women. There were three women who asked me out, who I then dated, none of which lasted long for various reasons. It had nothing to do with emotional conflicts, more due to circumstances and priorities. There was sex with those relationships and I had no problem with that. Maybe it's my Italian blood or something, or just the need to feel that emotion again. The sex was good.

It took me well over a year to finally feel good about the end of my second marriage and five or six years before I could say it was actually out of my system. I had no desire for a relationship, even though, as I mentioned, I did date. It was the total emotional attachment to that last marriage that made it hard to get over—all that I had given up for her came with a heavy emotional cost.

I called my first wife and wanted to meet with her. This was after many years but, out of guilt, I never showed up. I drove by the homes of both of my ex wives, just out of curiosity, but that sort of thing never helps. I have Googled both of their names but in the case of my first marriage, I have no idea what her married name is now and my second wife changed back to her maiden name and that never comes up when I do a search. I've looked through Facebook and Twitter but found nothing—again, the curiosity factor. Strange though, I'm all over those social media networks, including writing a daily blog and a couple of books but no one from my previous marriages has ever contacted me.

The most embarrassing thing I did was bringing my lover to meet my first wife at our house. OMG! That WAS stupid and I have no idea why I ever did that. To top it off, in front of my lover, my wife asked me who I loved and I answered my lover. THAT was embarrassing and stupid and boy, do I ever regret doing it!

What I would say to my ex's if I could:

To my first wife: Sorry we did not have the maturity of mind to work things out. Holding grudges after all these years is rather silly and I wish we could just be friends and chalk up the past as mistakes made on both parts. Sorry.

To my second wife: There IS nothing that could be said. Even though it's been over fifteen years since the divorce, she remains unstable, hostile and revengeful—even to the point of distancing herself from her own children.

As for soul mates, yes I think there are such things and I have actually found one and have been with her for more than ten years. We aren't married…living in sin. I would like to be married but things are going so great for the both of us, so why change it?

> ***Love is unconditional, relationships are not.***
> *Grant Gudmundson*
> *about.com Quotations*

42 Straight

I am married with children. I have a great job, good friends and consider myself to be very fortunate. My marriage isn't perfect but is there a perfect marriage? I love my wife and together we have a good life.

When I was a young man, before I married, I was with a woman, Charlotte. She was a beautiful girl. I was twenty-seven and she was twenty-one. I remember feeling like our age difference seemed like a lot at that time. Looking back, maybe it was but now that I am older, it's only six years.

We were together for a little over a year. It was a blind date set up by my friend. When I saw her, I was immediately attracted. She was as well. Of course I liked the fact that she liked me. If I called, she answered, if I asked her out, she was available. She was always available. I took her for granted and I did see other women while I was with her—mostly dates but nothing serious. Charlotte was my main squeeze. If I needed or wanted her, she was there and she gave me space if I needed it.

She was in college and very bright. She had her own life with friends and activities outside of our relationship. I did love her but she was too available for me and at that time I was too young to see value in that.

Eventually, I went on a date with someone else and became very interested in this other woman. The other woman was more of a challenge. She was older and I wanted to conquer her. Charlotte became less interesting to me and I eventually broke things off with her. She was very upset. She cried and begged me to reconsider. I felt bad but I had made up my mind. I moved on.

The relationship with the older woman was short lived. I did consider calling Charlotte but thought it wouldn't be the best idea. I had been kind of a jerk. I knew I had hurt her. So even though I thought of her from time to time, I went along and dated.

About two years passed and I found myself thinking about Charlotte more and more. I finally contacted her. She seemed genuinely happy to hear from me and we caught up. She told me about her new job and some other stuff about her life. I asked her to dinner and she told me she had a boyfriend. It was strange how when I heard those words come out of her mouth, I felt uncomfortable. Because she had always been there for me, I assumed nothing had changed. I assumed she would melt when I called.

I understood though. So much time had gone by. But I found myself jealous. I made a stupid joke that if and when she broke up, not to lose my number. God, I regret saying that. I must have sounded like an ass.

She was always the picture of grace and didn't say anything to make me feel stupid. We exchanged email addresses and hung up.

The more I thought about it, about her and what kind of woman she was, I regretted the way I was with her. She is a quality woman. I hurt her because I was too full of myself to see it.

Several more years passed and I met my wife. I would hear from Charlotte through email on holidays. She would send me a quick note wishing me well. She still does. She is now married and has children of her own. Every time I see an email from her in my inbox, I wonder if I'll be surprised, if she'll tell me she isn't married anymore. I don't know why. I am not unhappy in my marriage and cannot imagine leaving my wife. But I think of Charlotte often. I wonder what my life would have been like if I had given her more credit. More of a chance. I was young and full of testosterone.

I did have fun sowing my wild oats. But as I age, I think of what may have been. I don't cry and I don't feel agony. I just think about her a lot. I doubt she has those kinds of feelings for me. I was an ass.

You never know what life will turn out to be. Maybe one day....

For all sad words of tongue and pen,
The saddest are these,
"It might have been."

John Greenleaf Whittier

33 Straight

I have only had two serious relationships in my life so far and the break up of the first one was devastating to me. We weren't married yet, though we were engaged. We didn't have any children.

It was hard for me because I felt like I was being utterly rejected as a person. She was bipolar and went through severe bouts of depression that would last for months. At those times she ignored me, wouldn't tell me she loved me and often left our apartment to stay with friends until she felt better. I felt like there was something wrong with me because she never discussed any of what was going on with her. She'd simply go to work one day and call me later saying, "I won't be home for a few weeks and I can't be around you for a while." No explanation, no reason, nothing. So I would assume I had done something to really upset her.

> *"It is estimated that 2 to 7% of people in the United States suffer from bipolar disorder. Almost 10 million people will develop the illness sometime during their lives. About half of these will never receive the correct diagnosis or treatment."*
>
> The Bipolar Handbook: Real-Life Questions with Up-to-Date Answers, Penguin 2006: Dr Wes Burgess

The breakup itself happened true to form. I went to work one day and came home to find her and her things gone. All I was left with was a note telling me she had moved to another state. I never heard from her again.

I didn't try to get her back. I assumed she wanted nothing more to do with me, given how she left. Prior to the breakup I did everything I could to convince her to stay with me. Her job was very stressful for her, so I told her I'd pick up a second one or even a third so she could quit hers for a while and rest. She did quit but she left before I had the chance to get hired anywhere else.

I expressed my pain by crying. This might sound like an exaggeration but it isn't. I was so heartbroken that I cried most of the day every day for nearly a month. I didn't talk to anyone about it because it hurt too much to even mention her name. For about six months I kept to myself as much as possible. I got a tattoo that says *I walk alone* as a reminder to never allow myself to get into another relationship because if I stayed single I could never be hurt like this again. I worked extra hours and drove around late at night because I hated going back to my empty apartment and cold bed. Everything was a reminder of the fact that she wasn't there anymore. I was very depressed and felt suicidal several times.

I sought therapy after the breakup. Most of the advice came down to trying to realize that her leaving had nothing to do with me. I could accept that idea logically but it didn't change how I was feeling and the feeling was what was killing me inside. So, in my opinion, it didn't work too well.

Later on, I found out she had gotten married. At first, it made me feel horrible and I felt like a loser for not moving on faster and there was this sense of being not good enough because she obviously found someone she thought was better than I was. Then I thought about the poor guy she married and how he would be dealing with the same things I did and I felt much better.

It didn't take me very long to feel all right about her being married. I just figured she probably isn't much different than she was with me and I know how miserable I was with her. I quickly realized I was much better off without her

It was three years before I got involved with someone again. I allowed myself to heal and recover as fully as possible before trying again. I knew jumping into another relationship would only make things worse for me. During those three years I abstained from sex. That was the longest it took me to get over a relationship and luckily, I've been able to get over them all.

I've fallen hard for a few women in my life and never got to have a relationship with them. It did depress me and I felt so unimportant. You know, the whole, "She doesn't even know I exist" thing. I managed to get over them by slowly taking my focus off of them. I allowed myself to realize with each of them that she isn't the only woman in the world. I also chose to believe that if we didn't have a relationship it's because we weren't meant to.

To the ex who left me so coldly I would say I now know how much pain you were in and how hard it was for you to love yourself. You never felt good enough and you took that out on me. It was hard for me to feel so rejected by you as often as I did but I see now how much we both needed to have the experience of that relationship. You taught me a lifetime's worth of lessons in a few years. I have grown and matured so much because of that and I thank you for what you gave me. I only hope that you have learned to grow from what you learned from me. I wish you all the best in your life.

I believe in the concept of soul mates but as yet, I haven't met mine. I think it's possible to have more than one and that we learn from different people throughout our lives and that often comes from having relationships with multiple people.

I would like to get married because I love the idea of two people making such a strong commitment to one another.

We learn our greatest lessons from the ones we love the most. When love is painful don't forget that you're growing. Take heart and know that things will be better on the other side.

41 Straight

I doubt my story is unique. I was with Janelle for six years. We weren't married. I planned on marrying her but I wanted to do it right. I wanted to have a decent wedding and it has taken a while for my business to take off. We discussed this and planned to wed.

One day, she announced was done. She told me she didn't love me and that she was leaving. I was shocked. It seemed to come from nowhere. She never even sat down with me to talk about what she was going through. Looking back on it, I can see the little things that added up. She became more involved with other things and people, went out with her friends, got involved with her work and grew away from me.

It hurts a lot. She left me seven months ago but it feels like yesterday. At first, I drank a lot to dull the pain, though drinking made it worse and I admit I was doing some drunk dialing. She heard me out once but after that she didn't answer her phone. The one time she answered, I cried like a baby. I begged her to please give me another shot. She was polite and let me carry on but then she told me it was best not to call her anymore.

Perhaps if I were younger, I would be doing more destructive things like drinking and fighting. I don't drink too much now. Fighting wouldn't solve anything; it would only be a way for me to take out my anger on some poor slob who didn't deserve it. I am too old for that. I do work out. That helps to release some of the pent up energy I have but nothing takes away the hurt I feel.

I keep it to myself. You can't go on and on to other guys about how you feel. They don't want to hear it. So I just suck it up. I work really hard and find anything I can to keep me occupied. She creeps into my mind several times a day. I'll be at work, talking with clients and be thinking of her the whole time.

> *According to a recent survey, 57% of single people say thoughts of their ex prevent them from finding a new partner.*
>
> singlemenforwomen.com

I haven't dated anyone but I know that time is coming. I must find my way out of my own self-pity. I expect that initially it's going to suck. The whole dating thing repulses me. Meet a woman, take her to dinner, play the stupid game. I am not in the mood to be chivalrous or dashing. I want to stay home with my girl, watch movies, have sex, have breakfast with someone I know well and love. I had that and now it's gone. The whole idea of starting over seems daunting and exhausting.

I don't look her up on social media. There is no point. I think about her enough as it is. I haven't and won't see a shrink. Breakups happen and I have to deal with it.

The worst part is Friday and Saturday nights when I lie down to go to bed. I often have trouble falling asleep on those nights. She broke my heart. I have no anger for her and I do want her back. I don't delude myself in thinking she will change her mind. I did in the beginning.

I don't know if she is seeing anyone else and don't want to know. I think it would kill me to know if she was.

I really can't think of anything I would say to her. If I thought of something that would change her mind, I would. She told me she doesn't feel in love with me anymore. Words cannot change that.

Soul mate theories are a waste of time. A romantic notion that makes breaking up worse. She left me. It hurts. A lot.

76 Straight

I met my Grace when I was in the first grade. Her parents were immigrants from Europe and we sat next to each other in class. I can't say we were friends then but we knew each other. Our town was small and our class graduated each grade together.

When we were fifteen, our school had a dance and I asked Grace. Fortunately for me, she agreed. This was a real coup, as Grace was the first in our class to develop breasts and all of the boys wanted to go out with her. She was a great beauty, always the picture of elegance and containment. The air of mystery that surrounded her was intriguing to all and I was the lucky man who won her heart.

We married as virgins when we were both eighteen. We had a small ceremony with family and friends and for our honeymoon we took a trip to The Grand Canyon. It was all I could afford with my meager salary as a gas station attendant. Both of our parents pitched in as well, so we took a week.

Soon after our return, I started working for her father in the manufacturing business that eventually afforded us a very nice lifestyle. We purchased a home and Grace became pregnant with our first child at age nineteen. Soon after, we had our second child. This pregnancy was very difficult for Grace. She spent the last three months in bed and the doctors feared for her life. As it turned out, the second child came in less than two hours of labor without a hitch. Because that pregnancy gave us a scare, we decided not to have any more children.

My life with Grace was wonderful. We had a storybook marriage. I started taking her for granted though. I took to drinking and gambling with my buddies. I never strayed in our entire marriage but I did think that I deserved to go out to play. I made the money; I should be able to blow off some steam. This all started in about year three. Grace expressed her disdain for my activities but I told her she was my wife and her place was to take care of the children and keep a clean home. I have to admit when I write this I laugh at my sheer stupidity.

One day I came home from work, expecting my dinner to be ready and on the table like every other night. What I found instead was a note letting me know that Grace and our kids had moved out. She didn't say where she went but I knew she had gone home to her parents. I was irate. I showed up to her parents' home angry and insistent that she get back home right away! When her mother opened the door, she informed me that Grace was not with them. She went somewhere and wished to not hear from me again. My mother-in-law was cold and polite. After she shut the door, I stood there for what seemed like an eternity. I was confused and could not for the life of me figure out where my family could be. Little did I know, Grace was indeed with her parents and had witnessed this exchange from an upstairs window. She informed me much later that she had no real intention of leaving me, providing I saw the error of my ways.

I went home to a dark, empty house. I made a peanut butter and jelly sandwich and drank a bunch of whiskey. I fell asleep on the sofa and woke up hung over and late for work. Her father informed me that if I was a real man I had better get my shit together or I would find myself without a job as well as without a family. I secretly cursed him and for the next week I waited for Grace to come home. She didn't. Within that week the house started to become a complete mess. I didn't even know how to wash the clothes. The dishes started to pile up along with the dust balls.

When Grace showed up a little over a week later, at the time she knew I would be getting home, she told me that if I ever spoke to her in that condescending tone again, she would take the kids and leave for good. I was so happy to see her and I begged for her to return. Not only had the house become a disaster, I realized just how much I loved her and didn't want to be without her or my family. I stopped drinking and gambling. I promised I wouldn't take her for granted and after that, I never did.

My love for Grace deepened over our fifty-three years together. She became more than my lover, my wife. She was part of me and she took care of all my needs. Because of her and her love, I have come to see that women are the stronger sex, emotionally speaking. I can't count how many times, I would feel broken or defeated and Grace found the strength for me. She always knew what to say to make me feel strong without emasculating me.

Five years ago she was diagnosed with a terminal brain tumor. It all came on abruptly. Her whole life, she was the picture of health. The kids would fall ill or I would and Grace seemed to be immune to whatever ailed any of us. Then all of a sudden her health started to fail. When we got the news, the doctors told us she only had about three months to live. This news was devastating to me. I had always hoped that I would be the one to pass first, out of pure selfishness and fear. I couldn't imagine my life without her. She was my love, my rock and she helped me to be the man I am today. Two months later, I had to bury her and that was the most painful day of my life—harder than the day she passed.

My children and other family members were there for me for a few weeks after she passed. But then came the day everyone had to return to their lives, families and work. I found myself all alone in our home and on that day I seriously considered taking my own life. It would have been easy. I take heart medication as well as a few other medications to keep me going. I figured I would take them all and drink a bottle of Jack. As I drifted off to sleep that evening I believe Grace came to me. She told me to be strong and not to worry, soon enough we would be together again and until we were, she would be there to watch over me. I have felt her presence many times and even though it's something I can't prove, I know she is there.

> **Death leaves a heartache no one can heal, love leaves a memory no one can steal.**
>
> *From a headstone in Ireland*
> *quotegarden.com*

The next six months were the loneliest and coldest I have ever lived. Every night I would cry myself to sleep. Every morning I would wake up and feel I had nothing to live for. I talked to Grace all the time. I begged God to take me. I did try to involve myself with activities but often neglected to follow up. I just sat in my chair, ate TV dinners and mourned my great love.

I decided, at my daughter's prodding, to move into a senior retirement community. The big house was too much for me and the memories of my life there with Grace were too strong. This was the best decision I could have made. There is so much going on and so many people to help take the edge off. I also like to volunteer my time when I have the energy and it is how I came to find your request for my story.

Within five months of moving here, I met a wonderful woman who has helped ease the pain. She lost her husband about the same time I became a widower so we have that in common. We also both have two children and enjoy a good game of Twenty-One. I have come to love her and I believe she loves me too. But I think both of us still miss our respective mates.

I hear the term soul mate and if we have them, mine is Grace. I was a lucky man to spend my life with the woman who I loved dearly. I take pride in the fact I was loyal and treated her with respect—after she set me straight that is.

The pain of loss is so overwhelming. In my case, I doubt I will ever really get over her. She was my life. I no longer cry myself to sleep but I think of her everyday. Sometimes I am hit with a surge of emotion but I take comfort in the knowledge that we will be reunited and I must remind myself how lucky I am in the first place to have lived my life with her.

I am still in pretty decent health, knock on wood, but I know my days on this earth are limited. I am enjoying my time here but I do long for the day when I can be with her in heaven. I know she waits for me. I try every day to be worthy of her love when I make the transition.

I thank you for the opportunity to tell my story. I think this is an interesting idea for a book and I imagine mostly women will wish to read it. I'd like to say to you women, stand firm. If you are with a man who isn't treating you with respect, get rid of the bastard. Find someone who will cherish you and be worthy of being cherished. Our life is short. Before you know it, you're old. Find love. Find someone who has your best interest at heart and do not settle for less. I wish the authors of this book great success.

Afterword

As we noted in the beginning of this book, we aren't experts when it comes to the psychology of the male psyche. However, that doesn't mean we don't have opinions and observations of our own. The recurring theme throughout the accounts of the men who responded, as well as from the experts in their fields who were kind enough to add their commentary, was that men in our society aren't allowed to show or discuss their feelings in meaningful ways. They are often admonished to "suck it up". Indeed, for some it's a matter of pride to do so.

In the course of assembling the accounts, we came across several news articles that provided food for thought and we felt a little commentary of our own would be a good way to end this book and give you, the reader, something to think about.

First, and completely unrelated to anything having to do with heartbreak, is the recent discovery that repeated head injuries suffered by National League Football players are having dire effects. The recent death of former NFL lineman Shane Dronett is the latest in a string of postmortem findings that players, particularly lineman, have suffered irreversible brain damage most likely caused by concussions sustained on the playing field. The NFL is in the process of changing rules regarding going back into play after getting hit hard enough to feel symptoms of concussion. But there are players who are against the new rules and subscribe to that old "suck it up" mode of working through the pain. Former NFL quarterback Kurt Warner, in an interview with CNN, stated that nobody came right out and said that the players had to play whether they were 100% or not but there was always the fear that the other guys were looking at you and thinking you weren't being "tough" enough. That, we think, is a microcosm of society's (at least American society's) attitude where men are concerned. They are to be strong at all costs, whether it's physical or emotional pain.

Which brings us to the emotional side of things. An April 2011 Time article titled *Love Hurts* by Alice Park presents some startling data. Her sources are impressive: PNAS, FDA, Society for Health Care Epidemiology meeting and Environmental Health Perspectives. Working with forty individuals who had recently suffered romantic rejection, researchers found that pain experienced from heartbreak ignites the same sensory pathways in the brain that are engaged when an individual experiences physical pain.

This poses an interesting question. If emotional pain is suppressed rather than expressed, can long-term physical health be negatively affected? If someone suffers a heart attack and doesn't receive treatment, the problem is only worsened and takes its toll on the body. When a man is physically injured, he seeks medical attention. There is no shame in that. Yet, there is a sense of shame when admitting emotional vulnerability. We ask: Is it possible that not expressing or working through the pain of heartbreak actually causes physical damage to the body? Studies have proven that stress causes physical ailments. Heartbreak is a form of stress.

Many men who shared their stories noted they suffered in silence for years, even decades. Some men admitted to not having sex for years after falling victim to a broken heart. Even though this is a very small sample, there is no question that millions of men feel and react in a similar fashion to the stories we collected.

It would be nice to think that we can make this observation, pose this question and VOILA! Knowledge is power! Men will now get on the phone with their best buddies and cry and analyze and express the pent-up emotions they have held down for so long. Of course, that's not going to happen. But perhaps, with these findings and some time, men will come to realize the importance of sharing their feelings. It isn't weakness. It's important for mental as well as physical health. Just because you can't see it doesn't mean it isn't there.

Discussion Questions

- Has reading the stories changed the way you think about how men deal with breaking up?

- Who do you think has a harder time dealing with a broken heart? Men or women? Why?

- Where there things in the book that surprised you?

- There was a story about a Marine who received a Dear John letter while he was serving in Iraq. What are your views about breaking up in that fashion?

- Why do you think society discourages men from openly expressing their feelings?

- Why do you think gay men have an easier time expressing their feelings?

- Would you prefer to see men speak more openly about how they feel?

- There was a story of a married man who fell in love with another man. What are your thoughts about that? Do you feel he should stay in his marriage or admit that he is in love with a man? Do you feel it is fair to his wife to keep it from her? Do you feel he's being fair to himself?

- The last part of the book notes that the body responds to heartache the same as to physical pain. Do you think this new information will change the way men deal with their emotions?

Find us on the Web

Facebook:

Author Ann Werner
Author Kimberley Johnson

Twitter:

MsWerner
authorkimberley

Our Web site:

Arkstories.com

Made in the USA
Charleston, SC
20 May 2011